Michigan P

109 W. Michigan Ave., Suite 900
Lansing, Michigan 48933
1-800-292-5923

PARENTS ARE TO BE SEEN AND HEARD

KEY: ADV.0002A   TYPE: 380

Parents Are to Be Seen AND Heard:

Assertiveness in Educational Planning for Handicapped Children

Geraldine Ponte Markel and Judith Greenbaum

Impact &&& Publishers
POST OFFICE BOX 1094
SAN LUIS OBISPO, CALIFORNIA 93406

Copyright © 1979

Geraldine Ponte Markel and Judith Greenbaum

All rights reserved under International and Pan-American Copyright Conventions. No part of this book may be reproduced, stored in a retrieval system, or transmitted in any form or by any means, electronic, mechanical, photocopying, recording or otherwise, without express written permission of the authors, except for brief quotations in critical reviews, or for quotations from other sources hereby gratefully acknowledged.

Library of Congress Cataloging in Publication Data

Markel, Geraldine, 1939-
   Parents are to be seen and heard.

     Includes bibliographical references.
      1. Handicapped children--Education--Planning.
2. Assertiveness (Psychology)--Study and teaching.
I. Greenbaum, Judith, joint author. II. Title.
LC4019.M28   371.9   79-12924
ISBN 0-915166-28-3

Cover design by Sharon Schnare

Impact ॐ Publishers
POST OFFICE BOX 1094
SAN LUIS OBISPO, CALIFORNIA 93406

ACKNOWLEDGEMENTS

During the development of this text, materials were field tested with parents on an individual basis and in workshops sponsored by parent or professional organizations. A special thanks to these parents and professionals for their time and contributions.

We would like to acknowledge the assistance of the staff at Milan Middle School in Milan, Michigan. We are especially grateful for the support of Mr. Kenneth Spurr, principal, and special education teachers Carol Schuster and Phillip Downs who also contributed his skills as photographer.

The University of Michigan has also provided support for this endeavor. Historically, the Program in Special Education, Speech and Hearing Sciences has shown a commitment toward parent-teacher communication and cooperation. Many of the ideas, problems and examples surfaced during a community based practicum and seminar course, Family and Community Life of the Handicapped Child, which was directed by Judith Greenbaum. Percy Bates Ph.D. in conjunction with a parent group initially conceived of and supported this unique course and trainees have interacted with almost 100 families having handicapped members during the last nine years.

The assistance and encouragement of the University of Michigan, School of Education's Office of Instructional Services under the direction of Donald E. P. Smith Ph.D. with the technical assistance of Adelaide Harris is also appreciated.

TABLE OF CONTENTS

Foreword	ix
Introduction	1
Part I. Assertive Behaviors	9
Part II. Verbal Behaviors	21
Part III. Nonverbal Behaviors	35
Part IV. Listening and Note Taking	55
Part V. Legislation	71
Part VI. Problems and Strategies	87
Part VII. Skill Development	117
Conclusion	133
Appendix A: Answer Keys	135
References	143

FOREWORD

A tragedy and a courageous act is found embodied in the concept of Parents are to be Seen and Heard. One asks oneself, "Why must there be separate and special appeals toward effective interactions with school personnel?"

The school administrator and the school teacher command positions of authority in any community. Often instead of being the servant of the community representatives who appointed them, school personnel assume a role of omnipotence which relegates parents to the position of a visitor rather than encouraging them to be a participant in the educational process. Parents feel outside the school, rather than a part of it. The decade of the 1960's saw many changes in social attitudes in the United States which were essentially initiated by young people of college and high school ages. They demanded a part in decisions which affected their lives. Parents saw what was happening and gradually became active as well.

It is an interesting experience to observe school people attempt to withstand parents. It is often sad to observe the hostility of educators who should be assuming the leadership position in the community. These statements are directed at the majority of educators. It is not a matter of a small minority. Parents have seen themselves as a minority in the community of education rather than being in a position to suggest, oversee, and control a program which is the most fundamental of all aspects of government and democracy. Parents of "normal" children have demanded to learn how to work with school people, and, as with other minority groups, have assumed the need for assertiveness training.

Historically the education for handicapped children has been much worse. The handicapped child was not wanted, and was more often separated than integrated into the community life. Parents, filled with guilt, confused by problems of which they knew not, and confronted by hostility in the special school and by local school administrators, fought to maintain their own emotional integrity in the face of what were often insurmountable odds. In a careful survey done in a large New York State community in 1948, 46 children of school age were found hidden in their parents' homes in the city. These children had never been officially excluded by the public school system, nor were they known to twenty-six social agencies which operated in the same community. Parents, when asked why this situation existed, generally made comments reflecting on the hostility of school personnel toward their problem or stated that they were fearful school people would take their handicapped children from them. In the early 1940's when the National Association for Retarded Citizens, the United Cerebral Palsy

Association, Inc., and other smaller parent groups were organized, the situation began to change. In 1963 the Association for Children with Learning Disabilities was organized and another immense group of parents joined the other groups in demanding what was right for their handicapped children and youth. Parents, not the professional people, took the initiative. "But how does one effect change?" asks a parent. Parents were in a new arena, and were involved in activities with which they heretofore had had no experience. They found school officials, community leaders, the law, and the clergy often as opponents; too rarely as allies.

The parents have done a noble job, and some educators have also risen to the occasion. At the federal level P.L. 94-142 provides a basis for real services for handicapped children, but to date it has not proven effective. In contrast, general educators are often taking a strong position against the law. Little or no planning in the communities has taken place through which handicapped children could be integrated into the normal educational facilities. The very educators who thirty years ago fought against special educators and insisted that general education could better serve the handicapped, now in the 1970's are insisting that these children be removed from the regular grades! Something is amiss, and it is not the handicapped child. Good examples of normalization of handicapped children within the schools are hard to find, although a few exist.

To counter the forces of hostility directed toward the handicapped individual, parents and others have seen the need to become assertive — a role historically they have rarely played. If unfortunately such a role is demanded of parents, then guidance in operating within this new arena must be provided. The book which Geraldine Markel and Judith Greenbaum have prepared goes a long way to meet this pressing need. The book can be used as a guide by parents for actions within their communities, their schools, their state legislatures, and departments of education in behalf of their handicapped children. It should be pointed out that assertive action requires training in assertiveness. Any of us would prefer to see leadership accept its rightful responsibility and lead. When educational leadership does not perform in this positive manner, then parents must lead. The Markel-Greenbaum book is an important contribution to this new leadership. Through it, parents and others can learn how to obtain effective interactions with school personnel. Without parents who are knowledgeable, handicapped children will continue to be deprived of their birthright in spite of the law and in spite of the concept of education for all children.

William M. Cruickshank
The University of Michigan
Ann Arbor, Michigan
1979

INTRODUCTION

We live in a culture where nonassertion and conformity are valued. Proper manners, politeness, agreeableness, being soft spoken, not displaying anger, even our desire to dress in the current fashion assure that we do not stand out from others. We are also socialized to accept authority "without question." The principal says, "I have forty years experience as an educator." The teacher says, "I have a degree in mental retardation." The psychologist says, "I am a certified psychologist, and I feel this child should be institutionalized." In our society we are brought up to believe that these people must know more than we, that what they say is fact, and that despite our inner questions and concerns, we should respect "authority" and blindly follow.

It is difficult to break out of the double tradition: conformity and obedience to authority. And it is particularly difficult to do this gracefully and effectively as parents of handicapped children during interactions with school personnel. Assertive skills will facilitate an active parent role in conferences or personal interactions with school officials as well as with community or political groups.

This instructional program is designed to increase awareness and skills in specific school situations which have been identified as problematic by parents. It is not designed as a panacea for all the problems faced by parents in the schools. All case material is drawn from actual situations reported by parents.

The assumption underlying the program is that the parent wants to be perceived in the following ways.

- at the beginning of a conference: friendly, open, and interested
- during the conference: coping, controlled, credible, and capable
- at the end of the conference: respected and successful.

The primary goal of most of us, however, is not necessarily to be perceived well by others but to interact effectively with others. These two goals are interrelated but must not be confused as being one and the same. If one is too concerned about the perception of others, one ceases to act assertively and effectively.

Formal and informal groups of people, whether parents or professionals, often build up a mythology about themselves and the rest of the world which bears little relationship to reality. This mythology, if confused with fact, can interfere with the effective interchange between members of each group. For example: If a teacher comes to a meeting believing that "everyone knows that all parents are overemotional and impossible to work with," that teacher will not be able to work effectively with a particular parent. If a parent comes to a meeting feeling that a particular teacher "is known to dislike parent interference," that parent will not be able to work effectively with the particular teacher.

Each must try to begin a conference with a clean slate, ignoring the gossip and rumors circulated by his/her own group. At the beginning of a conference each party should assume the good faith of the other and the joint commitment to one goal: effective educational planning.

The materials presented here are designed so that parents can use them independently at their own pace. Many of the situations depicted illustrate negative behaviors on the part of professionals. Although parents experience many successes, this material examines those situations which are most frequently difficult to deal with.

The point of this training is to assist parents who have handicapped children to learn that the major source of help for their child resides within themselves. The exercises are designed to help parents become aware of their rights and develop skills to help obtain the best possible educational program for their child.

A Case Study

Please read the following true account:

I am the parent of four children, the youngest of whom is retarded and brain damaged. Like some parents, I wear two hats in relationship to the public schools, one as a professional educator and another as a parent of school children. Actually, I wear three hats: parent of three "normal" children, parent of a retarded child, and professional educator. If you are also the parent of a handicapped child, you will know that my experience is common.

In Michigan under the 1971 Mandatory Special Education Act, an Educational Planning and Placement Committee (EPPC) must be set up for each handicapped child. The EPPC must include the parent of the child. "Mandatory" ensures many other parental rights and is hailed as a giant step forward.

But when I go to an EPPC for my own daughter, I make sure to bring a friend. I have as much or more education as the professionals attending the meeting: I am middle class as they are, and white, and I certainly know my way around the public school system. I've lived here for 27 years. But I feel cowed when I go to the EPPC. I often feel that what I am being given is charity, not my right. I feel guilty because my child is very disturbing in school, and I feel that I am a bad parent. In turn, I get angry, defensive, apologetic, aggressive, and nervous. I don't mean to say that the professionals caused all these feelings. I certainly bring some negative feelings along with me, either from past encounters with professionals or from the remnant of guilt that many parents of handicapped children feel. We always worry: Have we done enough for that child? Have we shortchanged our other children? However, the professionals often add to the problem.

A description of one experience may be helpful. When my oldest son was in kindergarten and I went for parent-teacher conference, I was excited and pleased to go. The teacher told me, "Your son is exceptionally bright. He has many friends, and it's a pleasure to have him in class. I've looked forward to meeting you. You must be a marvelous parent." However, when my daughter Susanna, our retarded shild, was five and in kindergarten, I was nervous and tense before the conference. Indeed, I was told, "Your daughter can't stay in kindergarten. Maybe she could attend for just an hour a day. What? You don't agree with that? Are you just trying to get rid of her? Do you think we're just a baby sitting service?" I felt guilty, angry, and defensive. I was perceived as a poor parent. How could both these incidents have occurred to me? Did I really switch from being a model parent to being a poor parent? Is there something that professionals are saying, inadvertently, to parents of handicapped children — that we are less valuable than other parents? My experience is not unique.

Please answer the following questions by circling <u>yes</u> or <u>no</u>.

Do you feel and act like an assertive parent? To find out, circle the answers to the following questions:

1. I feel comfortable and at ease when I am at a conference with school personnel.　　yes / no

2. I ask questions if I don't understand a term or procedure.　　yes / no

3. I make direct requests for services or options that I feel are necessary.　　yes / no

4. I refuse to accept plans or suggestions that I feel are inappropriate or inadequate for my child.　　yes / no

5. I tell others at a meeting if I feel angry or disappointed.　　yes / no

6. I feel that my child is entitled to the special services that meet his or her needs.　　yes / no

7. I feel that my opinions are respected by school personnel.　　yes / no

8. I tell others at a meeting if I am pleased with or appreciate their efforts.　　yes / no

9. I feel that I look and act self-confident during conferences.　　yes / no

10. I feel that conferences result in plans that are appropriate for my child's needs.　　yes / no

If you have more than two "no" answers, you may benefit from assertiveness training.

Identify times you have felt or acted in a nonassertive manner.

_____
_____
_____
_____
_____
_____
_____

Describe the manner in which you would behave in each of the following situations.

You are at a school meeting but no one requests that you share your ideas or offer your opinions.

You are confronted by a teacher about the ineffectiveness of your management of your child.

An administrator has shown very considerate and supportive behavior towards you.

At a conference, the administrator and teacher agree on a course of action. You disagree.

It is the end of a conference. You feel unsure but you are being pressured by others to make a decision.

A teacher is not fulfilling his responsibilities as outlined in the I.E.P.

The administrator is describing aspects of the legislation which you don't understand.

You feel that the support services provided for your child are inadequate.

Problems

Parents who feel frustrated, hostile, anxious, and/or uninformed are at a loss when faced by the educational system. They often say that they see their situation as controlled primarily by forces outside themselves. They have neither authority nor power. They feel either that they are not responsible for their child's education or that they cannot significantly influence the content and direction of their child's special program. They feel powerless, incompetent, guilty, and angry.

Sometimes parents feel that professionals view them as "bad" parents. They feel that they are viewed negatively: as poor, divorced, black, disinterested, or aggressive. In other instances, parents see luck (if only we lived in another part of the state or had a different teacher) as the critical factor in obtaining services for their handicapped child. These views or underlying assumptions of the individual's powerlessness to have an effect on the system restrains them from acting effectively.

"The parent today is usually a coordinator without voice or authority, a maestro trying to conduct an orchestra of players who have never met and who play from a multitude of different scores, each in a notation the conductor cannot read. If parents are frustrated, it is no wonder: for although they have the responsibility for their children's lives, they hardly ever have the voice, the authority, or the power to make others listen to them." (Kenniston, 1977)

Action is necessary to provide the dynamic and productive thrust for change at this time in history. Parents, like other consumer or minority-status groups, should learn that they can be responsible for a significant portion of the decision making that occurs within the system and that self-determination for themselves and for handicapped individuals is as much their right as it is for any human being. The legislation (P.L. 94-142, The Education of All Handicapped Children Act, Section 504 of the Rehabilitation Act of 1973, and the Family Educational Rights and Privacy Act) specify and guarantee this, and the behavior of parents as individuals and as members of political groups will determine the fulfillment of the promises made by such mandates.

This is not to imply that the people one knows are not important. Quite the contrary. Knowing influential people is often essential. Therefore, the parents' strategy should be to acquaint themselves with those who have decision-making power and influence: principals, school board members, legislators. Parents as individuals and as members of community groups should arrange opportunities for such persons to know, like, and trust them. Parents must become teachers of these decision makers. Parents who feel that they can act assertively are more likely to initiate such interactions. They are more willing and able to bear the responsibilities that accompany the difficult and long-term changes demanded by recent special education legislation and related litigation.

If timing is a factor affecting success, then such current governmental and judicial events have provided the optimal climate for initiating change and allowing for the input of parents into the educational system. Assertive skills can facilitate an active parent role in conferences or in personal interactions with school officials as well as with community or political groups.

PART I. ASSERTIVE BEHAVIOR

Introduction

Assertiveness training for parents of handicapped children involves learning a set of social skills which, in turn, allows parents to express personal feelings, maintain their rights — both personal and legally guaranteed — and meet the educational needs of their children. It facilitates and insures the parents' involvement in the planning and evaluation of educational alternatives.

Assertiveness training is based on the premise that social behavior is learned. Since it is learned, with new training and practice inappropriate behavior can be unlearned and replaced by more appropriate and satisfying responses. Thus, if a parent has developed a set of responses related to school environments or interactions with school personnel and is dissatisfied with the results, he/she may learn other more effective behaviors.

During training, a set of responsible interpersonal behaviors is identified to help the parent interact with administrators, teachers, and others in a comfortable and effective manner. Systematic training focuses on assisting parents in identifying their rights, practicing assertive behaviors, becoming aware of the anxieties which inhibit assertive action, and decreasing their emotional anxiety through active practice exercises. Parents thus become more aware of their individual behavior patterns in dealing with school personnel and learn to practice alternative styles.

KNOWING YOUR RIGHTS

Your child's educational needs must be met. But this may not happen if your are not assertive. Being assertive means exercising your rights. You can't exercise your rights — either personal or legal — if you don't know what they are:

- some are basic human rights
- some are granted by Public Law 94-142
- some are implied by local, state, and federal guidelines
- some are granted by the Rehabilitation Act of 1973 (Section 504)
- some are granted by the Family Rights and Privacy Act

Let's first read through them. Later we shall look at examples of situations where these rights were violated.

Basic Human Rights

- the right to ask for and receive explanations from professionals
- the right to function in the role of parent as one does for all one's children
- the right to refuse inappropriate requests or pressures without feeling guilty, selfish, or ignorant
- the right to express opinions and be heard with the same respect and consideration accorded others
- the right to lobby singly or in groups for changes in existing laws and for creation of new services necessary for the education of the handicapped
- the right to "shop around" for the kind of professional advice and evaluation the parent respects and considers appropriate for the child
- the right to hope and work for some improvement in the child's functioning without being told that the parent does not accept the child's "limitations"

Some of the rights granted to parents by federal law, The Education of All Handicapped Children's Act (P.L. 94-142), are as follows:

- a free and appropriate public education for handicapped children between the ages of 3 and 21
- an Individualized Education Plan (I.E.P), written with the participation of the parent, for each child on a case-by-case basis
- implementation of the I.E.P. in the "least-restrictive environment" for each child. This means that, depending on his/her strength and needs, the child should be placed with "normal" children as much as possible
- a diagnosis of the child made in his/her native language or "mode of communication" on a racially and culturally nondiscriminatory basis
- an opportunity to examine all school records pertaining to the child
- a due-process procedure so that, if they disagree with particular programming or placement decisions, parents can challenge these decisions. The law specifies a series of steps available to parents to do so (called "due-process")
- an annual evaluation of each I.E.P.
- a State Advisory Board constituted by each state to include parents, teachers, and handicapped individuals

Some rights implied by local, state and federal guidelines include:

- the right to have prescribed procedures followed as outlined in legislative or school manuals
- the right to know about and observe, first hand, available services or facilities
- the right to help plan the best program for each child
- the right to help decide priorities and schedules
- the right to make the ultimate decision ragarding the child's placement within the limits of the law

Section 504 of The Rehabilitation Act of 1973 became effective in 1977. This act prohibits discrimination on the basis of handicap in employment, education, transportation, housing, and any other services receiving financial support from the federal government. This act provides that:

- all programs offered by a school district to its nonhandicapped children must be accessible to all children
- at least some school buildings in each school district must be accessible and barrier free to handicapped persons
- handicapped children cannot be segregated from the general school population by being placed in one school or classroom
- academic adjustments and adaptations in the manner in which courses are conducted (as well as testing procedures) must be made to accommodate the needs of handicapped children
- where major architectural changes are necessary, the school district is given up to 3 years to comply

The Family Rights and Privacy Act provides that:

- parents of a student under 18 years of age must be permitted to inspect and review all records maintained by the school district
- if the parents feel that some information in the record is inaccurate or misleading, they may place in the records a statement commenting on or disagreeing with that information
- the only people who have access to the records are those within the school system who have a "legitimate educational interest" in the particular student's record. A record of access must be kept of all persons who have viewed a particular record
- parents must give written consent for the release or transfer of the records to someone outside the school system

ASSERTING YOUR RIGHTS

The nonassertive parent will either (a) apparently agree with all that is said, or (b) not participate in the discussion and/or decision making. In both cases, the professionals will make the decisions. In both cases, the child may suffer.

Assertion

In each situation (Exercises 1, 2 and 3), choose the assertive parent response. Circle a or b.

EXERCISE 1

Problem/right: The parent is being asked to play a role other than parent – i.e., administrator, teacher, etc.

Situation: The parent has made a request of the principal.

Principal statement: I wish you could see it from my point of view. We have 15 other students in that class and your child is just one of them.

Parent response:

a. I guess if I were doing a better job at home this wouldn't happen. I don't know what to do.

b. My role is that of a parent, not that of an administrator or principal. My main concern is my child. Yours is management of the class.

EXERCISE 2

Problem/right: The parent has the right to ask for an explanation.

Situation: A psychologist is talking to the parent at an evaluation and placement conference.

Psychologist statement: I have reviewed John's tests, and he is emotionally disturbed.

Parent response:

a. Please explain the tests and what they mean.

b. "Oh my God," parent cries, and runs out of the room.

EXERCISE 3

> Problem/right: The parent has the right to refuse inappropriate requests.
>
> Situation: The child has had an extensive battery of tests by experts contracted by the parents. School personnel seems to differ with recommendations by these consultants.
>
> Psychologist statement: We'd like to have some additional testing done. I'm sure you will give your permission.
>
> Parent response:
>
> a. Barbara was just seen by a neurologist two months ago, but I guess it wouldn't hurt.
>
> b. I see no need for additional testing at this time. Barbara was seen by a neurologist only two months ago.

In these examples, the nonassertive responses show parents accepting the school's view or blaming themselves for the situation. These reactions may foster parental guilt, anxiety, and often avoidance or aggression at a later date. Nonassertion is also observed when parents do not provide appropriate praise or appreciation to school personnel. It is important to provide information to administrators and teachers about the helpful things they do that are especially meaningful to you. The chances that they will continue to do such things are greater when they receive positive feedback from you.

Nonassertion

When parents are nonassertive they allow others to violate rights generally ascribed to competent adults in addition to those rights guaranteed by law. The administrators, clinicians, or teachers act as the primary decision makers for the child, and the parents are only minimally involved in program selection and design.

Nonassertive behavior is observed when the parent allows a placement to be finalized without fully understanding the diagnostic findings or the rationale for the placement. Nonassertive behavior may be a direct result of the intimidation and inadequacy parents often feel in the presence of professionals. The nonassertive parent accepts the programming recommended by the school. Sometimes he/she quietly withdraws from future interactions with educational personnel (forgets or cancels conferences) or passively resists programs or procedures designed at school conferences (loses papers or keeps the child at home).

Negative consequences are attached to these nonassertive behaviors. The school may erroneously continue to perceive itself as the primary decision maker and continue its condescending attitudes while carrying out its "charitable" acts. The parents may be labeled as unknowledgeable, uninvolved, or neglectful. The school may then feel that it is legitimate to reduce or cease attempts at further communication and involvement of the parents in any decision making.

As a result, the parents may feel hurt, angry, or frustrated and may subsequently work in indirect, hostile, and emotionally dishonest ways. A negative cycle evolves and continues. The result tends to be inadequate or inappropriate programs for the child.

Nonassertion is seen when parents do not provide direct compliments to individuals who have helped them and whose actions they appreciate. Nonassertive behavior is also observed when parents deny, protest, or show embarrassment when a teacher or principal compliments them.

EXERCISE 4

Circle the assertive parent response.

Situation: The principal has consistently supported the requests of the parent. This has created some tension between the director of pupil personnel and the principal.

Parent response:

a. The parent tells a friend, "I should tell the principal that I really appreciated his help."

b. The parent tells the principal, "I want you to know that I really appreciated your efforts on my behalf."

EXERCISE 5

Circle the more assertive parent response.

Situation: The teacher and the parent are walking into the conference room.

Teacher statement: We really enjoyed the cookies you brought for the class party. They were great.

Parent response:

a. No, really, it was nothing. I was baking anyway.
b. Oh, thank you. I'm glad that you enjoyed them.

EXERCISE 6

Circle the appropriate parent response.

Situation: At the conference the parent has explained her goals for her child as best she could. The Director of Special Education at one point asks the parent a series of pointed questions which helps the parent clarify her thoughts to the group.

Parent response:

a. Thank you for your help. Your questions really helped me clarify my thoughts.
b. The parent says nothing.

Assertion vs Aggression

When parents are aggressive, they stand up for their rights by attempting to impose their beliefs and choices on other decision makers in the school. In doing so, they violate the rights of others. Their aggression may be openly hostile or more indirect.

By law, the schools are charged with and should be accountable for the educational programming of handicapped children. Teachers and administrators have a legitimate right to recommend and suggest objectives, schedules, priorities, and program options. Parents who attempt to get their way during conferences by yelling, insulting, and dominating others usually foster feelings of anger and humiliation which in turn present barriers to effective communication and collaboration. Parents should simply state their position.

Circle the assertive parent response in exercises 7, 8 and 9.

EXERCISE 7

Situation: The parent has requested additional help in reading for her son.

Principal statement: That may be a problem. We only have one reading therapist.

Parent response:

a. Johnny is entitled to this type of service. He has some special needs.
b. If you were more efficient, you'd have more time for Johnny's special needs.

EXERCISE 8

Situation: The psychologist is discussing a diagnostic report with a parent.

Psychologist: These tests indicate that Bill doesn't understand much about what is going on around him.

Parent response:

a. I'm very upset about your report. Would you please explain these tests.
b. How dare you say that! You only spent one hour with him and you think you know all about him. Of course he knows what's going on.

EXERCISE 9

Situation: Prior to the meeting, the teacher, Mrs. Wilson, agreed with the parent that the child should be placed in a special class each morning. The principal disagrees with this idea.

Principal: Mrs. Wilson and I have agreed that under the circumstances a regular class placement with supportive services is the best alternative for Jill.

Parent response:

a. Mrs. Wilson, I'm disappointed that you changed your mind after agreeing that Jill should be placed in your special class each morning.
b. Mrs. Wilson, YOU TRAITOR. You've no backbone. You know you said Jill needs a special class.

In these situations, the parent who responds aggressively blames the school personnel for the problem or "tells them off." This action usually fosters more hostility and a cycle of negative interactions.

Sometimes the aggressive feelings of parents are shown in indirect ways. The parent may attempt to attain objectives by trickery, manipulation, or acting in a "two faced" fashion. The parent's hostility towards or frustration with school personnel is expressed in ways that may provide some short-term revenge but usually also result in a long-term pattern of negative, nonproductive interactions. The consequence is often less than ideal programming for the handicapped child. The needs of the child are overshadowed by the gamesmanship of the adults. Parents who act in indirectly aggressive ways are late, forget important appointments, lose papers provided by the school, or make school personnel look incompetent or foolish by exaggerating their mistakes or by gossiping about them.

EXERCISE 10

Circle the assertive parent response.

Situation: Mrs. Copeland is furious with the note which was sent to her by the principal. Her next conference appointment is at 4:00 p.m. on Wednesday.

Parent behavior:

a. Mrs. Copeland keeps the principal waiting and arrives at 4:45 p.m. She says that she wrote down the wrong time.

b. Mrs. Copeland arrives at 4:00 p.m. and privately discusses her feelings about the note with the principal.

Short-term gains may be achieved by aggressive behavior, but in the long run, school personnel may respond by avoiding such confrontations and hostilities and by working in ways which, for all practical purposes, exclude parental involvement. Neither aggressive (direct or indirect) nor nonassertive behaviors provide the critical conditions needed for systematic and effective program planning. However, both types of behaviors are fostered when parents feel either that they do not have legitimate rights or that they are helpless in attaining such rights.

Assertive behavior is a direct, honest, and appropriate expression of one's feelings, opinions, and beliefs. Parents who act assertively communicate actively and stand up for their rights in ways that do not violate the rights of others. At a conference the parent expresses opinions and feelings in a forthright and confident manner. The parent participates in a team effort and is responsible for the final acceptance of a program. Assertive behavior is demonstrated when the parent asks questions about tests or terminology used as a basis for placements. For example: A psychologist describes test scores that the parent does not understand. The parent who is assertive might say, "Would you please explain how these results and scores were obtained?"

Circle the more assertive parent response in Exercises 11 and 12.

EXERCISE 11

Problem/right: The parent is being stereotyped and not dealt with as an individual. The parent has the right to be treated as a capable adult and not to be patronized.

Situation: The teacher is responding to a request made by the parent during a conference.

Teacher statement: Now, Mrs. Burton, you're being too emotional. Most parents feel this way. way. You're so involved with your own child that you can't make the best judgement for him.

Parent response:

a. I feel that I have legitimate concerns about my child and this program. I hope you will listen to my concerns as this child's mother, not as an "emotional" parent.

b. You're lazy and just want to get him out of your class.

c. Well, I guess you're right.

EXERCISE 12

Problem/right: All children are entitled to educational services.

Situation: The parent called the principal for information on the class schedule for the winter semester.

Principal statement: We've reviewed your son's file and feel he can graduate next semester. However, because of his special problems he doesn't have to come to school. We'll just send the certificate in June.

Parent response:

a. I realize that Bill has been fighting a lot recently and he has been difficult to handle. I'm really sorry he's caused so much trouble.

b. I'm not going to listen to a ridiculous story like that. You're an idiot. I'm going to call the superintendent.

c. The state guidelines are very specific in that all children are entitled to educational services. My son is no exception.

Summary

Nonassertive behavior is interpersonal behavior which allows the parent's rights to be violated. In allowing others to violate one's rights, desired goals are seldom achieved. On the other hand, aggressive behavior, whether direct or indirect, attempts to fulfill rights at the expense of others. Neither type of response is apt to foster a continued, positive team approach to a problem. The problem and the child are often lost in such interactions.

The assertive response attempts to focus objectively on a clarification of a law or role or on a description of a feeling, a nonconfronting, nonblaming description which centers on communicating information in an acceptable way. It is a more business-like response because it indicates control and task orientation. Assertive responses are an attempt to continue discussion of viable alternatives rather than to close discussion with name calling, emotional outbursts, or acceptance of plans that the parents do not understand or like.

PART II. VERBAL BEHAVIORS

The exercises in Part II are designed so that the scripts may be audio-taped. If tapes are not made, you may read these scripts yourself or have someone act them out.

Introduction

Our verbal messages can be categorized as nonassertive, assertive, or aggressive. Classification of a verbal message is dependent upon the meaning of the words as well as the manner in which the words are spoken. The fashion in which a message is presented will communicate feelings to the listener and have an impact on the direction of the discussion.

Listen to (or read) the interactions at school conferences between parents and school personnel. Circle the type of response given the the feelings which are communicated by the parent. Identify the effect the message might have on the discussion.

Exercise 13, Script A

Psychologist: I have tested John and find that he falls into the mentally defective range.

Parent: Mentally defective? You saw my child for one hour and you call him defective? He is not defective. (Said in anger, loudly, glaringly.)

EXERCISE 13

Script A

1. The parent's response is:
   a. assertive
   b. aggressive
   c. nonassertive
2. The message expressed by the parent is:
   a. anger
   b. anxiety
3. The parent is:
   a. insulting
   b. questioning
4. The effect of the message would be to:
   a. continue discussion
   b. discontinue discussion

Exercise 14, Script B

Psychologist: I have reviewed the reports and evaluations concerning Bill and have come to the conclusion that he is a very emotionally disturbed boy.

Parent: I just don't feel comfortable with your statement. Tell me how you arrived at that conclusion. (Said in well modulated, clear voice, conversational tone and adequate volume.)

EXERCISE 14

Script B

1. The parent's response is:

    a. nonassertive

    b. assertive

    c. aggressive

2. The message expressed by the parent is:

    a. anger

    b. challenge

3. The parent is:

    a. sharing feelings

    b. insulting

4. The effect of the message would be to:

    a. continue discussion

    b. discontinue discussion

Exercise 15, Script C

Situation: The parent has made a request of the principal.

Principal: I wish you could see it from my point of view. We have 15 other students in that class and your child is just one of them.

Parent: If you were more efficient you'd have more time for Johnny's special needs. (Said in angry and loud tone.)

EXERCISE 15

Script C

1. The parent's response is:

    a. aggressive
    b. nonassertive
    c. assertive

2. The message expressed indicated:

    a. anger and blame
    b. resignation and fear

3. The effect of the message would be to:

    a. continue a problem solving positive discussion
    b. discontinue a problem solving positive discussion

Exercise 16, Script D

Principal: I wish you could see it from my point of view. We have 15 other students in that class and your child is just one of them.

Parent: I realize that you try to meet the needs of all children. However, I would like you to consider the special needs of John at this point. (Said in a well timed, firm tone).

EXERCISE 16

Script D

1. The parent's response is:

    a. aggressive
    b. nonassertive
    c. assertive

2. The message is:

    a. empathic, requesting
    b. complacent, nondemanding

3. The effect of the message would be to:

    a. increase a problem solving discussion
    b. decrease a problem solving discussion

Exercise 17, Script E

Psychologist: After carefully examining the findings of this case, I recommend that the child be institutionalized immediately. You must accept the fact that he will never improve.

Parent: He is only five years old. He is part of our family. We want him to remain at home with us so that we can help him as much as possible. An appropriate school placement will help. (Said in a whining, higher pitched manner)

EXERCISE 17

Script E

1. The parent's response is:

     a. nonassertive
     b. assertive
     c. aggressive

2. The message communicated is:

     a. challenge
     b. intimidation

3. The effect of the message would be to:

     a. increase a problem solving discussion
     b. decrease a problem solving discussion

Exercise 18, Script F

Situation: School is being dismissed. The parent is meeting her child. She has come from work, is exhausted and has a headache.

Teacher: Mrs. Wilson, do you have a minute? I must speak to you about Karen's behavior.

Parent: I know that you are concerned about Karen and would like to deal with this today, but I'm not up to it right now. Can we make an appointment in a day or two? (Said with feeling, calmness and moderate rate)

EXERCISE 18

Script F

1. The parent's response is:

    a. assertive
    b. aggressive
    c. nonassertive

2. The message is:

    a. whining and negative
    b. empathic and positive

3. The effect of the message would be:

    a. to decrease the discussion of alternatives
    b. to increase the discussion of alternatives

Even a word which seems to have a single and clear meaning may be communicated in a variety of ways (Exercises 19 and 20). The impact of the word will be dependent on the volume, speed, and pitch of the voice.

Exercise 19, Script G

Situation: The principal is making a request of the parent.

Principal: We can not provide transportation for John to and from school. We may be able to pick him up on the bus in the morning. Can you have him picked up at school in the afternoon?

Parent: Ah . . . no. You see I uh don't uh have a car and uh . . . (Said in a soft, quiet tone, with several hesitations)

EXERCISE 19

Script G

1. The parent's voice was:

    a. too soft
    b. too loud

2. The parent's voice was

    a. too fast
    b. too slow

3. The message was:

    a. assertive
    b. nonassertive
    c. aggressive

Exercise 20, Script H

Situation: The Psychologist has made the following statement.

Psychologist: Suppose we arrange for Michael to be tutored at home by a teacher consultant. That way he won't be in class and apt to disrupt the other children.

Parent: No! (yells, high pitch)

EXERCISE 20

Script H

1. The parent's voice was:

    a. too highly pitched
    b. too low pitched

2. The parent's voice was:

    a. too loud
    b. too soft

3. The message conveyed by the parent was:

    a. assertive
    b. nonassertive
    c. aggressive

The pitch or frequency of the voice, as well as the loudness and speed of the presentation, will influence the message presented. In addition, the credibility of a message may be reduced if the words are accompanied with inappropriate sighs, stammering, or laughter.

Exercise 21, Script I

Psychologist: This is a very serious situation. Have you considered residential or institutional care?

Parent: Oh my god. No, I, I, just couldn't, I mean I wouldn't do that. (crying)

EXERCISE 21

Script I

1. Circle the word(s) which describes the parent response.

    a. credible
    b. noncredible

2. Write a credible and firm parent statement:

   _____
   _____
   _____

Exercise 22, Script J

Parent: My role is that of a parent, not of an administrator or principal. My concern is my child. I rely on your expertise to manage the class. (Consistency between the words and the delivery. The parent defines her role and concern. Voice is well modulated and calm.)

EXERCISE 22

Script J

1. The words are:

    a. assertive
    b. aggressive
    c. nonassertive

2. The delivery is:

    a. assertive
    b. aggressive
    c. nonassertive

Exercise 23, Script K

Parent: My role is that of a parent, not of an administrator or principal. My main concern is my child. I rely on your expertise to manage the class. (fast and loud, emphasis on my and your)

EXERCISE 23

Script K

1. The words are:

    a. assertive
    b. aggressive
    c. nonassertive

2. The delivery is:

    a. assertive
    b. aggressive
    c. nonassertive

3. The words and the delivery are:

    a. consistent
    b. inconsistent

4. Circle the words which describe the parent's delivery:

    a. too fast
    b. too slow
    c. too much stress on some words
    d. too little stress on some words

Exercise 24, Script L

Parent: The legislation is intended to provide all children with an education even if they are handicapped. (uneven fluency, stammer, whining)

EXERCISE 24

Script L

1. The words are:

    a. assertive
    b. aggressive
    c. nonassertive

2. The delivery is:

    a. assertive
    b. aggressive
    c. nonassertive

3. The words and delivery are:

    a. inconsistent
    b. consistent

4. The delivery is nonassertive because of:

    a. uneven stress on some words
    b. stammering
    c. tone of voice (whining)

Communication is a complicated process. If the parent wants to send a clear, credible, and firm message, his/her verbal behaviors (the words used, and the delivery of the statements) and nonverbal behaviors should be consistent. The same is true for school personnel. Sometimes they, too, show contradictory verbal and nonverbal behaviors. Parents are frequently faced with and confused or angered by administrators who give double messages. These inconsistencies are usually meaningful and should not be ignored. Whether or not the parent deals with the problem at that time is an individual judgement, but an awareness of the inconsistencies may help the parent plan his/her own actions.

Exercise 25, Script M

Situation: The Director of Special Education is talking to the parent.

Director of Special Education: Mr. Blair, I know your son has been out of school for eight weeks, but it is because we are putting so much time into planning the perfect program for him. You must be patient. (polite and well modulated voice)

EXERCISE 25

Script M

Circle the word which describes the director of special education.

1. The delivery of the message is:
    a. positive
    b. negative

2. The words provide a statement the meaning of which is:
    a. positive (Appropriate action is being taken.)
    b. negative (No services are being provided.)

3. This message shows a(n):
    a. consistency
    b. inconsistency

Once aware of inconsistencies, the parent may decide to confront the speaker and identify the discrepancies and the problems created.

EXERCISE 26

1. An assertive parent's response to the Director of Special Education (Exercise 25) would be:

   _____
   _____
   _____

Of course, inconsistencies on the part of school personnel may also involve their nonverbal behaviors, in which case the parent must process several cues at one time. A message can be very confusing when there is little unity between facial expression, body gesture, words, and delivery.

Think of your attempts to communicate at a recent conference or discuss your verbal behavior with a friend. List aspects of your verbal behavior that are effective and those that could be improved.

Verbal Behaviors

Effective Behaviors	Aspects to Improve
_____	_____
_____	_____
_____	_____
_____	_____
_____	_____

Summary

Our verbal behavior is a significant aspect of the total impression we convey to others. The words employed, as well as the manner in which they are delivered, influence others and the subsequent actions that evolve.

Assertive verbal behavior involves statements which are neutral rather than blaming or critical and a presentation in which a firm message is spoken in an even, clear, and audible manner. Inconsistencies between the content of a verbal message and the manner in which it is delivered, should be avoided.

PART III. NONVERBAL BEHAVIORS

Introduction

Much of our communication with others is nonverbal: The body has its own language and method of providing signals and impressions to others. A great deal of our body language is unintentional, and we are frequently unaware of the messages we send to those with whom we interact. In addition, our messages may or may not be consistent with what we say or do.

Nonverbal behaviors include posture, movement, distance from others, gestures, and facial expressions. Moods or feelings are often transmitted to others by the seemingly random activity of our bodies. For example, anxiety or tension can be revealed in fidgety behaviors such as finger tapping, paper twisting, foot jiggling, trembling, nail biting, hair twisting, nonstop smoking, or excessive perspiring — all psychophysiological means of coping with anxiety or fear.

The nonverbal behaviors which communicate self-confidence and add credibility to assertive verbal behaviors are reflected in the parent's initial greetings outside the conference room as well as at the table during a meeting.

The initial greeting between the parent and teacher sets the tone for the day's interactions. Standing straight and shaking hands firmly rather than slouching and waving communicate a confident and businesslike attitude.

EXERCISE 28

Check the picture in which the mother greets the teacher in a more assertive manner.

___ a

___ b

36

Body posture indicates and should correspond to the feeling or message the parent wants to communicate to the teacher or other school personnel. A relaxed posture during conversation, rather than a stiff, tense, or rigid stance, indicates a firm and confident attitude.

EXERCISE 29

Check the picture in which the father (printed shirt) is in a relaxed standing position.

___ a 
___ b

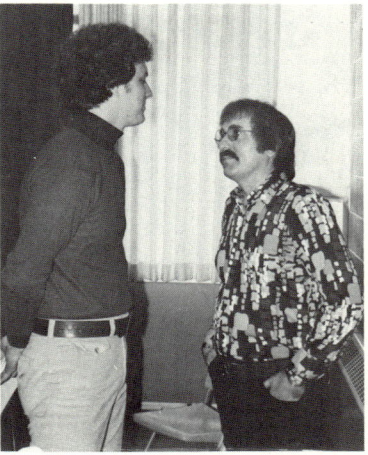

EXERCISE 30

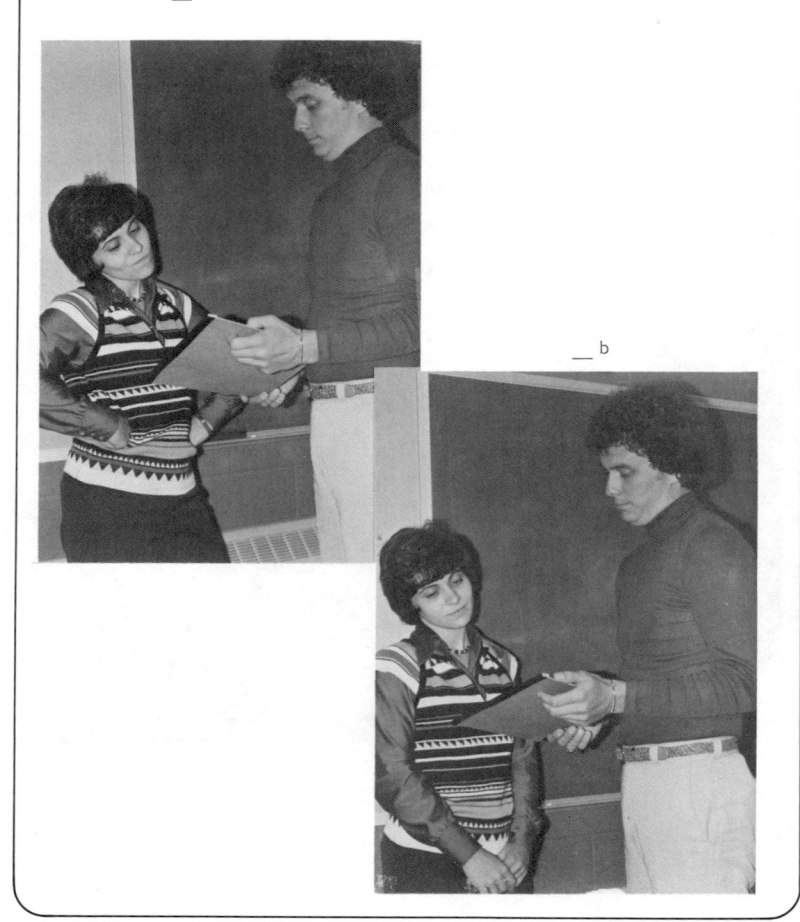

Check the picture in which the mother is in a relaxed physical stance.

___ a

___ b

EXERCISE 31

Check the picture in which the father (center) is in a relaxed body position.

___ a

___ b

39

The seating arrangement at a conference can encourage or hamper parent participation. Whenever possible, round conference tables should be used because they facilitate access to printed materials and foster more natural, on-going eye contact among group members. All chairs placed at a table should be the same height.

The parent should sit between other main decision makers, such as the principal and teacher. If a rectangular table is used, the parent should sit on the side along with school personnel rather than off to one end alone. There is a greater likelihood that the parent will act and be treated as a team member when sitting within the group than when sitting alone at the end of the table.

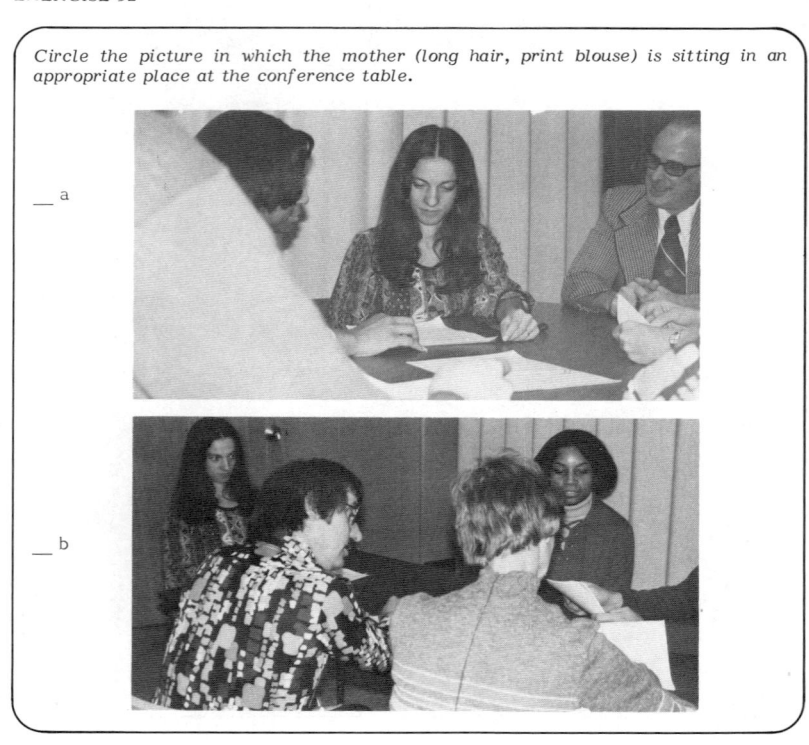

EXERCISE 32

Circle the picture in which the mother (long hair, print blouse) is sitting in an appropriate place at the conference table.

___ a

___ b

An advocate or friend often accompanies the parent to school meetings or conferences. The seating arrangement should allow for ease of communication and support between them. The parent or advocate should suggest a rearrangement of the seating if this does not occur.

EXERCISE 33

Check the more assertive nonverbal parent behavior.

Situation: The advocate (in the turtleneck shirt) is separated from the mother (back to camera).

___ a. The mother motions the advocate to move the chair next to hers.

___ b. The mother is uncomfortable but stretches to show the advocate the papers.

Hanging one's head and averting eye contact can be interpreted by school personnel as signs of avoidance, nervousness, and lack of confidence. This nonassertive behavior can prompt others to ignore or take advantage of the parent. In addition, lack of eye contact often results in discomfort for others in the conversation. Holding one's head erect and establishing and maintaining eye contact are essential components of assertive parental behavior. They facilitate active participation and involvement and increase the comfort of others who are present at the conference.

EXERCISE 34

Check the picture in which the mother maintains a more assertive position.

___ a.

___ b.

42

Facial expressions connotate our feelings as forcefully as do our words. Taut forehead muscles, knitted eye brows, and tension around the neck, jaw, and mouth can indicate fear or hostility.

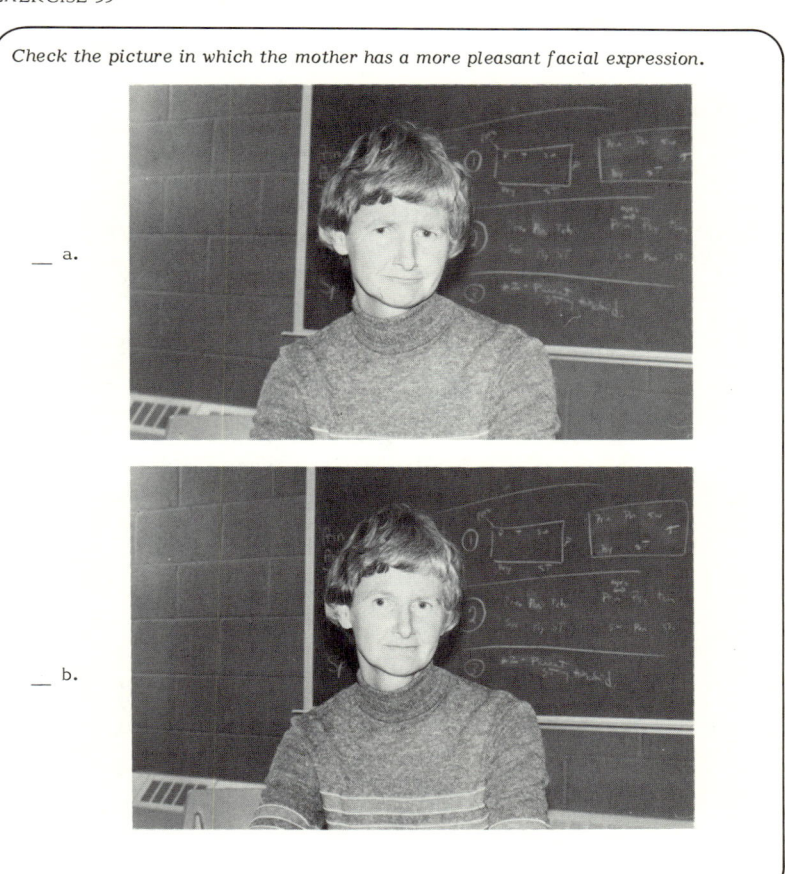

EXERCISE 35

Check the picture in which the mother has a more pleasant facial expression.

___ a.

___ b.

One's hands can communicate nervousness, embarrassment, or lack of control. Clenched fist, tapping fingers, and tightly folded hands can distract others, make them uncomfortable, and/or perpetuate the stereotype of the "emotional" parent.

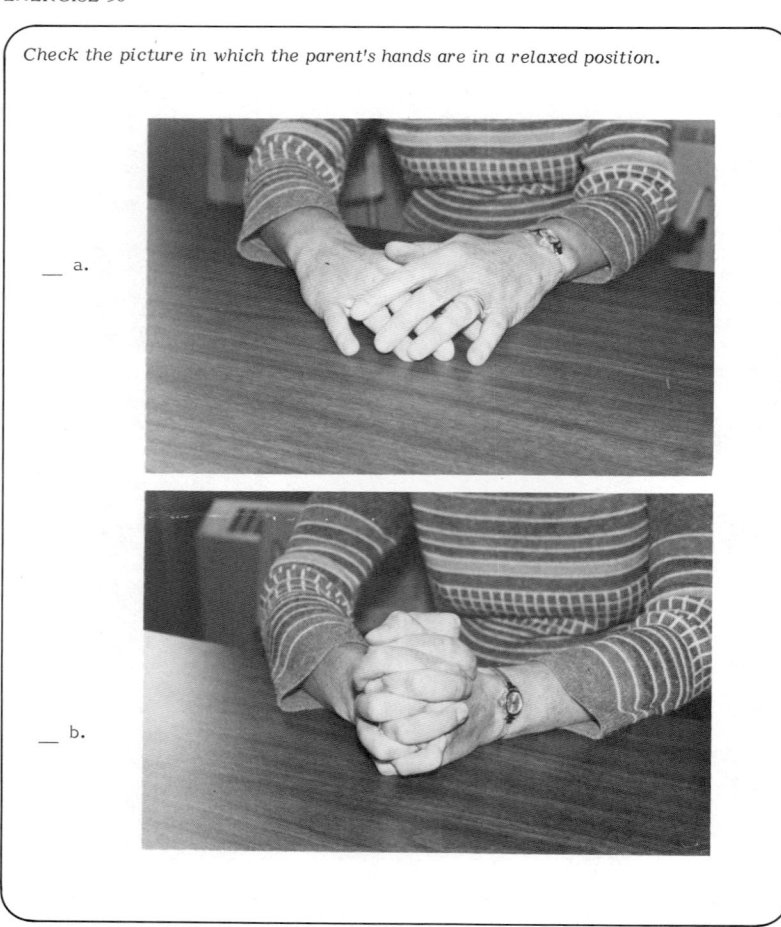

EXERCISE 36

Check the picture in which the parent's hands are in a relaxed position.

___ a.

___ b.

Assertive behavior is indicated by facial expressions that are attentive and businesslike. The parent can create this expression with a direct gaze, a listening expression, slightly forward tilted head, and perhaps moderate breathing through opened lips.

EXERCISE 37

Check the picture in which the mother has an attentive facial expression.

___ a. ___ b.

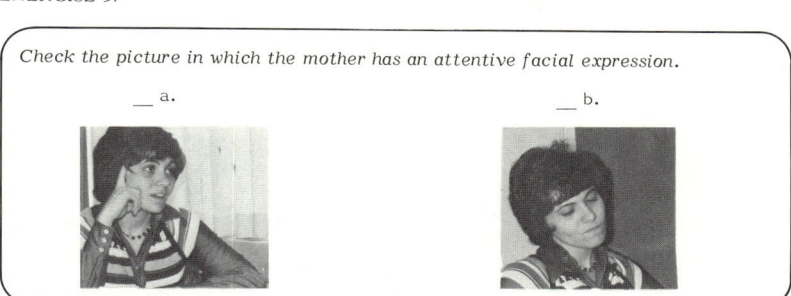

Keeping the hands in a relaxed position or engaged in purposeful activity, such as note taking, can help overcome the parent's initial uneasiness.

EXERCISE 38

Check the picture in which the father's hands give a more businesslike impression.

___ a. ___ b.

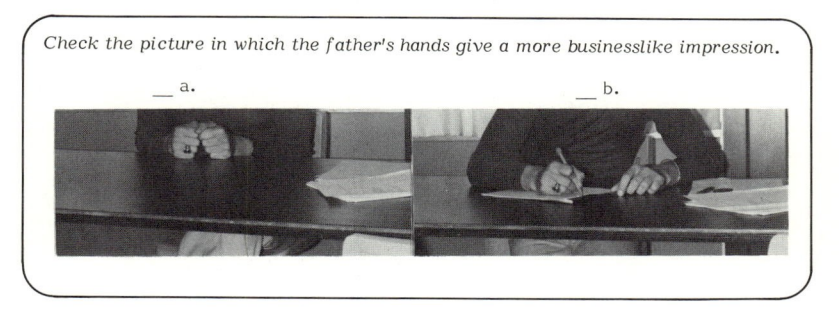

One's hands can support or negate other verbal or nonverbal behaviors. Covering the mouth when speaking or shielding the eyes when looking at others tend to hinder efforts towards assertive communication. Hands near one's face or in an open, relaxed position can increase the look of interest and involvement of the parent when conversing with school personnel.

EXERCISE 39

Check the picture in which the father is using his hand in a productive way.

___ a.

___ b.

Physical gestures can communicate our feelings and reinforce our verbal messages. Appropriate gestures provide or illustrate a clear message in an objective, nonemotional manner. Effective physical movement adds emphasis without hostility.

EXERCISE 40

Check the picture in which the mother is providing an appropriate physical gesture with her hands.

___ a.

___ b.

47

Rigid body positions and/or negative facial expressions provide signals to the parent or advocate that excessive anxiety or anger is present and that a change of pace may be useful. Once such tension builds up, it is too frequently reduced in unproductive ways (i.e., crying, shouting). To control such situations and to avoid unnecessary outbursts, the parent can suggest a break, identify his/her feelings, momentarily shift topics, or perhaps say something humorous.

EXERCISE 41

Check the picture which signals the need for the following statement: "I feel a bit tense. Let's take a five minute break and stretch a bit."

___ a.

___ b.

There should be consistency between the parent's verbal and nonverbal messages. Unity between facial expressions and words ensures that the person to whom you are speaking understands your feelings. Sincerity and commitment appear stronger if a serious facial expression accompanies a complaint and a smile appears with a positive statement. Descriptions of feelings should be communicated in an open, honest, and direct manner; smiles should not accompany angry or hostile messages.

EXERCISE 42

Check the picture in which there is consistency between the facial expression and verbal message.

I'm extremely angered by these remarks.

___ a.

I'm extremely angered by these remarks.

___ b.

EXERCISE 43

Check the picture in which there is consistency between the facial expression and the verbal message.

___ a.

"I am very pleased with this plan."

___ b.

"I am pleased with this plan."

Occasionally the nonverbal behaviors of school personnel show a lack of respect and are felt by the parent to be rude or demanding. Such behaviors include continuous shuffling of papers, not looking at the parent, interrupting the aprent, or ridiculing the parent's opinion. Sometimes such behaviors can be ignored; the parent may wish to highlight helpful and polite behaviors rather than make an issue of negative aspects of the interaction. However, if the behaviors annoy the parent and interfere with his/her effective management, the parent should be assertive, label the negative behavior in a calm and objective manner, and describe the feelings that this behavior creates.

On the other hand, teachers, principals and other personnel frequently have helpful and comforting nonverbal behaviors. A friendly gesture or touch can signal support and understanding.

Think of the last school meeting. Identify nonverbal behaviors of school personnel which were helpful and those that were irritating.

Nonverbal Behaviors of School Personnel

Helpful	Irritating
_____	_____
_____	_____
_____	_____
_____	_____
_____	_____

EXERCISE 44

Check the picture in which the teacher and social worker are paying attention to the mother's statement.

___ a.

___ b.

52

EXERCISE 45

Check the more assertive parent response.

___ a. I find it difficult to continue the conversation when I'm trying to make a point and your are not looking at me.

___ b. Please, please pay attention to me. I really need your help. You don't seem to be listening to what I'm saying.

Write an additional request for attention.

_____
_____
_____

EXERCISE 46

Check the appropriate parent response.

Situation: The principal is emphasizing a remark. The mother feels angry because he is pointing his finger at her.

a. Stop pointing your finger at me. Who do you think you are?

b. When you point your finger at me I feel uncomfortable.

Write another assertive response.

_____
_____

Picture yourself at a recent conference or discuss your nonverbal behaviors with a friend. List those aspects which are effective and those that could be improved.

Nonverbal Behaviors

Effective Behaviors	Aspects to Improve
_____	_____
_____	_____
_____	_____
_____	_____
_____	_____
_____	_____

Summary

Nonverbal behaviors are a major part of the total communication system which functions during interactions between parents and school personnel. Patterns of body movements, gestures, and facial expressions function as instructions to others about our feelings and attitudes and the effects others have on us.

Nonverbal behaviors can be classified as nonassertive, assertive, or aggressive sets of responses which may or may not be congruent with the verbal messages of the parent. Attention to and control of nonverbal behaviors can enhance the credibility and directness of the parent's message. An awareness of the influence of nonverbal behavior on others and a conscious planning and control of such behaviors should facilitate the parent's attempts to act and feel assertively.

PART IV. LISTENING AND NOTE TAKING

Introduction

Communication is a two-way process which involves receiving as well as sending information. Developing effective listening and note taking skills can assist parents to receive information more accurately, enhance their efforts to communicate, and help them become assertive in several ways:

- <u>Effective listening and note taking helps us gain more complete and accurate information</u> about the actions or feelings of others. Passive listeners tend to hear primarily what they expect to hear. With active and effective listening skills, we are more apt to hear what is actually said. Such information assists us in problem solving and program planning. Our confidence is increased since our strategies are based on fact rather than on guess or misinformation. Such strategies have a greater chance of success.

- <u>The more attention we pay to the speaker the less we concern ourselves about our own inadequacies or anxieties.</u> The more active and involved we are in the listening process the less chance that our minds will wander to other, less relevant topics.

- <u>Effective and attentive listening may provide a model for others</u> and increase the chances that they will listen to us.

Effective listening and note taking skills can be developed by asking and answering questions before, during, and after the conference. The use of questions facilitates the efficient collection and use of the information which is communicated by those at the meeting.

Asking questions helps us be active, rather than passive, listeners because it involves us in the speaker's message. This involvement increases our concentration on the information we need to gain or present. Before a conference, parents should write a list of questions to be answered either by themselves, the teacher, or other school personnel. Questions can be generated by:

- talking to the child, reviewing the child's work at school and his/her behavior at home

- reviewing notes or reports from previous meetings

- reading recent articles from newspapers or magazines that relate to your concerns about your child

EXERCISE 47

> Read the following newspaper article. Circle the question a parent might ask if the child were deaf and currently enrolled in a school program.
>
> **BY WILLIAM GRANT**
> Free Press Education Writer
>
> A small group of parents of deaf children last year asked the Southgate school system to set up a course for them in sign language.
>
> The school system obliged. In fact, says Stan Mazur, director of adult education programs in Southgate, "Give me 10 people who have an interest in anything, as long as it is moral and ethical, and I'll set up a course."
>
> The Southgate sign language course is one of thousands of adult education programs offered all over Michigan by virtually every public school system and community college.
>
> a. Why don't you people do what they're trying in Southgate?
>
> b. Are there any courses in our community which teach sign language to parents?

EXERCISE 48

> Read the article below and write a question the parent could ask the teacher or psychologist.
>
> # Hearing Loss Overcome By Vibrations
>
> BERRIEN SPRINGS (UPI) — At 17, she's all smiles and dimples and thrilled about being a cheerleader.
>
> Karen Loomis suffers from a profound hearing loss, which to most people means that she's deaf.
>
> But like thousands of other similarly handicapped children enrolled in public school systems around the state, Karen has been taught how to hear and how to speak.
>
> She's enrolled in a special education program whose director claims, "You're only deaf if you reject hearing."
>
> Sign language is not even taught in the program for hearing-impaired children in which Karen and many others in the Berrien County area learned how to communicate normally.
>
> The program is headed by Andrew Gantenbein, whose work in field of acoupedics — the stimulation of the ear's auditory nerves through sound vibrations — has become a showcase for the state.
>
> Karen said she used to be embarrassed by her deafness and hated the thought of being institutionalized. When she was younger, she attended the Michigan School for the Deaf 200 miles away in Flint and was taught to communicate by sign language.
>
> Though enrolled in the special program, Karen now attends classes with the student body at large and participates in such extracurricular activities as cheerleading — an accomplishment that makes her downright proud.
>
> Question to be asked by parent:
> _____
> _____
> _____

EXERCISE 49

Read the following school reports and meeting notes. Circle the question which would be most appropriate for the next conference.

School reports:

Psychologist's report 6/76 (Dr. Dunning):

... and according to the Wide Range Achievement Test, Judy had a 2.5 reading score.

Psychologist's report 10/77 (Dr. Young):

... a 3.5 reading level was attained on the Gilmore Oral Reading Test.

a. In what ways has my child improved in reading?

b. Is that good progress?

Parents might also ask the following questions:

1. What do these scores mean?
2. I notice there are two different tests. Is that important?
3. If my child reads at a 2.5 grade level in 1976 and at 3.5 grade level in 1977, does that mean that she has progressed one grade in reading in one year.

EXERCISE 50

Write a question that could be asked by the parent.

Situation: Billy scored 3.4 in computation and 1.0 in story problems on a mathematics test.

_____
_____
_____

Prior to a conference parents may have to review notes from several sources. These sources may include not only a school report but letters from physicians and the parents' own notes.

EXERCISE 51

Read the following notes and write 1-2 questions that a parent might bring to the next conference.

NOTES FROM TEACHER'S REPORTS:

10/78
"more manageable but no friends. Peter's miserable life."

11/78
"I've tried everything."

LETTER FROM SCHOOL:

Dear Mrs. Jenson,

We are very concerned with Peter's lack of progress. Peter has been in five previous placements which include special programs for the educable mentally impaired, trainable mentally impaired, multiply handicapped, emotionally impaired and a "normal" setting. We question if any of these have been appropriate to his needs.

This is a most complicated situation with a youngster who has many complex problems. It is obvious that he needs a consistent program geared to his needs. I doubt if Brown School can offer such a program.

NOTES FROM PHYSICIANS' LETTERS AND REPORTS:

9/73 Letter: Dr. Malcolm to Dr. Franks – Hospital
"Stigmata of autistic child" (neurological report).

11/72 Report by Dr. Water (psychologist) "rate of development slowed" "retardation questionable."

11/76 Report by Dr. Taylor (pediatrician) "normal" "normal eye examination" "autistic-like behavior."

PARENTS' NOTES TO SELF:

- Peter placed in five different programs within 2 years for children with different problems and needs.
- Peter is not progressing in school. School doesn't seem to want him.
- Some professionals call him autistic.

When parents enter a meeting with 2-5 questions they feel a greater involvement, purpose, and control. They can act assertively when they identify their own questions, request answers, or seek clarification of issues. Parents should do this even if difficult issues seem to be avoided or not spontaneously answered by professionals during the meeting.

EXERCISE 52

Circle the appropriate parent response(s).

Situation: A conference is half over, and the parent feels that important issues are not being raised and that questions which must be answered are being avoided.

Parent response:

a. I really enjoyed talking with you.

b. I've heard many good ideas today, but the question we must address is, "What educational program is to be set up for Bill?"

During the conference the parent should listen for the answers to those questions identified prior to the conference as well as to the questions that arise during the discussions. Notes should be taken on the answers, and the notes should be organized so that the information can be used at the end of the conference to summarize, check accuracy, or interpret conclusions. Because they are often referred to at a later date, the notes should be readable and accurate.

Good notes have the following features:
- <u>Information is written in blocks</u> or chunks. Space is left between each separate idea or related point of information to allow you to add pieces of information at a later time as various individuals speak.
- <u>Key ideas or words are written</u> rather than long sentences. The fewer words written, the more time available for thinking and processing information.
- <u>Space is provided on the left-hand margin</u> of the page for questions that are or should be answered.
- <u>Feelings, discrepancies, or issues are highlighted</u> by circling or underlining important words or phrases.

EXERCISE 53

> *Check the notes which will provide information in a more readable and useful form.*
>
> a. . . . says that Barbara wanders around the room, teacher doesn't know what to do. No concentration — Doesn't hand in assignments. There is a problem and it isn't going to go away.
>
> b. | What's the the problem? | Principal — Wanders around school.
 Teacher — No concentration. Not handing in assignments. |

EXERCISE 54

> *Circle the feature of good or efficient notes that is missing.*
>
> | What suggestions? | Possible programs:
 — regular preschool program
 — 2 days a week — outpatient clinic
 — speech and language therapy |
>
> a. block of information
> b. speaker's name
> c. question

In order to listen and take notes effectively, the parent must listen for the answers to questions. This is accomplished by listening for and identifying key words or phrases which can then be turned into a question.

60

Exercise 55 Script N

Principal: Good morning everyone. Well, it is certainly a nice day today. We are here today to discuss Kelly's program options for next year. We should be able to begin now. We have a lot to go over.

EXERCISE 55

Listen to (or read) Script N for exercise 55. Circle the key word or phrase in the principal's opening statement.

a. work and classes

b. program options

EXERCISE 56

Write a question using the key words from Exercise 55.

Exercise 57, Script O

Principal: Dr. West will begin. He recently tested Kelly and will present his findings and suggestions for program options.

Dr. West: I tested Kelly during May, 1976, and administered the revised edition of the Wechsler. She tested in the upper limits of the educable range. Her reading level is low, however, around 2.5, and her math level is about fourth grade.
 She needs help with money concepts and measurement (such as inches and feet, pints and quarts). Her handwriting is unreadable. I have been told that her vocational education placement is in food services.

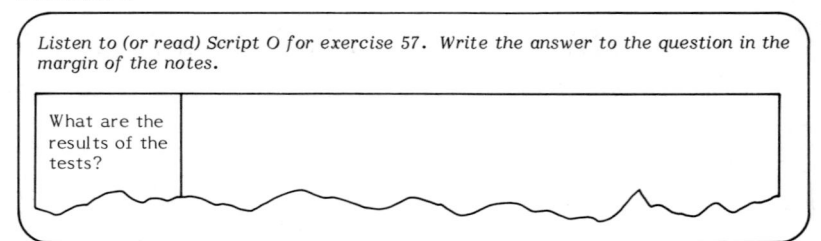

EXERCISE 57

> *Listen to (or read) Script O for exercise 57. Write the answer to the question in the margin of the notes.*

What are the results of the tests?	

Exercise 58, Script P

Psychologist: During our session Kelly showed good initiative and independence. She appears to have some visual motor problems. There are a few things I might suggest in terms of future programming. It would be interesting to find out if she has learning disabilities which would contribute to her difficulties in reading. I think too it is possible to continue a full time school program which would be a combination of academics and other courses. For example, typing, English and swimming. She certainly needs more mathematics this next year. This should include money management and measurement skills. We could try typing since her handwriting is so poor. This would help her to communicate better.

With her slight tendency to overweight, some physical education should be included. Kelly has indicated that she likes swimming.

Now, we could also consider placing her in a part-time job in the afternoon with some academics in the morning but I don't think that she's really ready for this.

EXERCISE 58

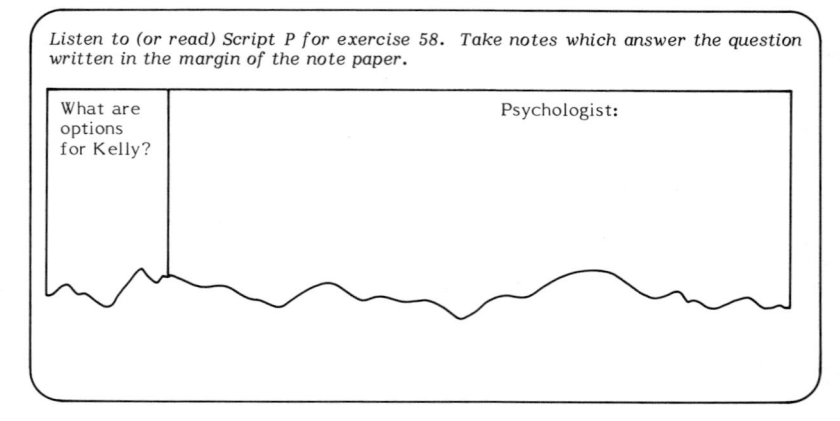

> *Listen to (or read) Script P for exercise 58. Take notes which answer the question written in the margin of the note paper.*

What are options for Kelly?	Psychologist:

It is important to organize the information provided by the various participants at a conference. This can be accomplished by writing one or more questions that are to be to be answered and leaving space for the answers provided by different people.

	principal	psychologist	teacher	parent
What is the most important problem?	unmanageable behavior in lunch room	feeling of inferiority	fighting in class	truancy
What has been done this year?	suspension from school	private therapy	exclusion from class	called school punished child

Exercise 59, Script Q

Psychologist: The most important aspect is testing for learning disabilities. This year I provided some counseling but that's not enough. The results of her Wechsler indicate that she is capable of reading on at least a fourth grade level and she isn't. We should find out the reasons for this by administering some additional tests.

Principal: In order for Kelly to graduate at the end of the year, she must take English and Speech. There is a scheduling problem. The times of the Speech and English classes conflict with typing. Therefore, she can't take a typing class.

Mother: I'm most interested in her learning to handle money. She can't make change for a dollar. How can she graduate from high school if she can't do this? I don't think she did much of this kind of activity this year.

Teacher: I think Kelly has learned all she can as far as money is concerned. And that goes for reading too. We did a unit on money this year. I feel the main problem is her lack of motivation.

EXERCISE 59

Listen to (or read) Script Q for exercise 59. Write notes on the form below.

	principal	psychologist	teacher	parent
What is the most important problem?				
What has been done this year?				

Taking notes effectively is difficult for many parents. A review of notes indicates that several common problems occur:
   a. too many notes
   b. too few notes
   c. omissions
   d. inaccuracies
   e. illegible writing
   f. loose information (pieces of information that are not tied to a topic)

EXERCISE 60

Circle any problems you had when writing notes to the above four exercises.

   a   b   c   d   e   f

Parents may bring a tape recorder to conferences and record the meeting. Such tapes reduce some of the problems involved in accurate and efficient note taking and provide an accessible permanent record of the interactions.

After a conference the parents should review their notes, specify problems, and set goals to improve their note taking in future meetings. A process involving self-evaluation, goal setting, and practice can yield more useable conference notes for the parent. After each conference notes should be edited, dated and filed for future access and use.

It is sometimes difficult to take notes during a conference because the speed of the speaker and the complexity of the message cannot be controlled. The parent has the right to request the speaker to repeat comments or modify conversational style.

EXERCISE 61

Circle the assertive parent response.

Situation: The principal is making opening remarks, and the parent is overwhelmed by the rate of his presentation.

Parent response:

a. Excuse me. Please slow down a bit. This seems to be important information; I want to be sure to get it down.

b. What? ... excuse me ... What did you say? ... What?

EXERCISE 62

Circle the assertive parent response.

Situation: The psychologist is proposing a very important step. The parents are concerned about his ideas and the legalities involved.

Psychologist statement: I think the parents must accept the fact that this child needs 24-hour-a-day protection in an undemanding atmosphere.

Parent response:

a. Oh.

b. I'd like you to rephrase your last statement so that I can be sure I understand it before I write it down.

A quick review of one's notes should be completed before the conference is adjourned. The parent may need to assert him/herself in several ways:

o ask for a minute or two to check the notes
o ask for clarification which will correct omissions or inaccuracies
o raise questions that were not answered — even if they must be answered in a future meeting
o read notes to the people in the group to see if they feel your notes are consistent with what they intended to say.

EXERCISE 63

> *Circle the assertive parent response.*
>
> Situation: Several topics were discussed during the last few minutes of the conference. The parent is concerned with the accuracy of the notes.
>
> Parent statement:
>
> a. I hope I wrote down the correct dates.
>
> b. I would like to read the dates back to you . . .

Parents may want to add a section to the notes concerning their own feelings or the reactions of others who were present at the meeting. These notes should be separated from the factual information.

On some occasions while taking notes the parent must stop listening and start talking. When others ramble, repeat, or change topics, the parent may feel it is necessary to interrupt the speaker and present his/her own ideas.

EXERCISE 64

> *Circle the more assertive parent response.*
>
> Situation: It is almost lunch time, and the conference began at 9:15 a.m. The teacher has been rambling and telling unnecessary stories.
>
> Teacher: Ah yes! I remember another time when . . . when I was a boy . . .
>
> Parent response:
>
> a. It's almost lunch time, and before we leave we must deal with the original topic — the need for additional physical therapy for my child who has cerebral palsy.
>
> b. Wow — it's late — I mean, well, I was wondering if perhaps we could, might talk a little bit about physical therapy.

It is important not only to listen efficiently but also to show others that you are paying careful attention when they are speaking. This attitude shows respect, provides reassurance, and helps avoid the tension or anger that builds when a speaker feels ignored. Whether intentional or not, nonattentive listening behavior can communicate coolness and distance towards others, which, in turn, tends to inhibit easy and productive communication. The listener can show attention to the speaker in both nonverbal and verbal ways.

Nonverbally the parent can:
- look at the speaker
- nod occasionally (when and if there is agreement) The parent must be careful not to nod if there is disagreement or confusion
- write notes concerning facts presented by the speaker

Verbally the parent can:
- restate the content or feelings stated or implied by the speaker ("you mean that . . .")
- ask a question ("are you saying . . ."?)
- make a confirming statement ("yes, I see, I understand")
- provide an example to support the speaker's statement

These techniques support the speaker and indicate that his/her message is understood. Without interrupting the flow of information, the speaker knows that the communication cycle is functioning.

Information gained during a conversation involves both content (statements, etc.) as well as feelings or emotions. The listener should show the speaker that the feelings as well as the content of the message are understood. The listener does this by reflecting back to the speaker the feelings that seem to be accompanying the content of the message. The listener can use phrases such as:

- "It sounds as though you're feeling . . ." or
- "I'm wondering if you're feeling . . ."

These comments may appear somewhat artificial at first, but they do indicate that you are attempting to understand, communicate, and collaborate rather than jump to conclusions or operate under needless minunderstandings. Sometimes it is necessary to separate the statements from the feelings or inferences discussed during the meetings.

Exercise 65, Script S

Teacher: Well, I have though about the situation and I don't think the child is benefiting from my program. (Not stated in an assertive manner – i.e., stammering, slow, very soft spoken).

EXERCISE 65

Listen to (or read) Script S for exercise 65. Separate the statement of the teacher from the feelings that are reflected. Circle the statement which reflects the feelings of the speaker.

a. I really want this child to remain in my class.
b. I really don't want this child in my class anymore.

The listener should consider asking for clarification when there seems to be a discrepancy between the speaker's content and feelings. A request for a description may also be indicated when the listener can't identify the feelings of the speaker or is confused by the message.

EXERCISE 66

Circle the more appropriate parent response.

Situation: The teacher seems to be making contradictory statements to the parent.

Parent response:

a. I'm confused. On the one hand you seem to be saying that you want my daughter to remain in your class, but on the other hand I get the impression that you feel she is disturbing you and the other children.
b. First you say one thing and then another. Can't you make up your mind? Do you or don't you want Lisa in your class?

EXERCISE 67

Circle the more appropriate parent response.

Situation: The teacher has telephoned the parent. This is the second call the parent has received in a month.

Teacher response: Mrs. Pen, I haven't seen you in a few weeks. Why don't you just come in for a little chat?

Parent response:

a. I am very busy this week. Is there something important you want to ask me or tell me about my son? If so, I will rearrange my schedule so that we can meet.

b. Oh my God, what's the matter?

c. How nice, I'm very busy this week, but it's so sweet of you to want to see me. I'll just drop everything.

Active involvement in listening does not necessarily involve a verbal response by the parent. Sometimes the parent listens and watches the professionals as they interact. The parent can take notes on the interchanges between others — these notes can provide information, insights, or cues on the content or timing of the parent's future behavior.

Exercise 68, Script T

Situation: The supervisor from the intermediate school district is whispering to the teacher while the Director of Special Education is talking.

Director: Will you two please be quiet? I find it very difficult to talk when others are distracting me. I'm suggesting a program for Frank, and I would like you to give me the courtesy of your attention.

EXERCISE 68

Listen to (or read) Script T for exercise 68 and circle the note the parent might jot down.

a. ... tension between director and staff

b. ... makes suggestions for Frank

Picture yourself at a recent school conference, attempting to listen and take notes or look at notes from past meetings. List aspects of listening and notetaking behaviors that are effective and those which should be improved.

Listening and Notetaking

Effective Behaviors	Aspects to Improve
_____	_____
_____	_____
_____	_____
_____	_____
_____	_____

Summary

Efficient listening behaviors which provide both information and insights can enhance a parent's communication skills. Listening skills are developed by asking and answering questions before, during, and after a meeting.

Practicing listening skills allows the parent to be more actively involved in interactions with school personnel and to collect notes. Such notes, comprised of facts and perceptions, then provide the basis for a more systematic planning of goals and strategy. A continuous review of notes provides the parent with an evaluation of events or patterns of behavior that have evolved. Notes provide a chronical of events and illustrate the degree of success a parent has gained in his/her attempts to attain an effective program for the handicapped child.

PART V. LEGISLATION

Introduction

The Education for All Handicapped Children Act (P.L. 94-142) is legislation passed by the United States Congress and signed into law in November, 1975. The intent of the law is to provide a free, appropriate public education which meets the unique needs of each handicapped child and to provide special education and related services in the least-restrictive environment.

- Every law has rules and regulations governing it which become part of the law. Guidelines are also written which explain the law in greater detail and suggest interpretations. However, they do not have the status of the law.

EXAMPLE FROM FEDERAL RULES AND REGULATIONS

§ 121a.5 Handicapped Children . . .

b.9 "Specific learning disability" means a disorder in one or more of the basic psychological processes involved in understanding or in using language, spoken or written, which may manifest itself in an imperfect ability to listen, think, speak, read, write, spell, or to do mathematical calculations. . . .

- The law is interpreted differently by different people and will be amended by act of Congress as the need arises as well as by judicial decisions resulting from civil action brought by individual parents and consumer groups.
- In addition to the federal law, each state has its own law regarding the education of handicapped children. The federal law sets the minimum standards required of every state if the state is to receive federal money to help it educate handicapped children. The state can set even higher standards for itself.

    Example: The Michigan Mandatory Code covers ages 0-25.

    The federal regualtions cover ages 3-21.

- Copies of federal and state law, rules and regulations and guidelines are available through your State Department of Education.
- An up-to-date knowledge of the rights, rules, and regulations and possible interpretations of the law is critical to the effective planning of programs by parents with school personnel.

The federal law uses several key terms relative to programs for handicapped children.

FREE = Education and related services are provided at no cost to the handicapped person or parent.

APPROPRIATE = So far this term is not specifically defined by law, and this situation presents great difficulties for both parents and educators. The term will have to be clearly defined before it can be used effectively in planning for handicapped children. However, one may attempt to deal with it by identifying gross discrepancies within the programming process.

EXERCISE 69

Circle the better parent response.

Situation: At the planning conference it was agreed that John was a learning disabled child as defined by section 121a.5 of P.L. 94-142. His school day was to be evenly divided between a regular classroom and a learning disabilities classroom. However, the school district has neither a trained learning disabilities teacher nor a classroom. The Director of Special Education suggests that John be placed in a class for emotionally disturbed children for half the day.

a. I have a concern about the costs involved.

b. I have a concern about the appropriateness of the placement.

EXERCISE 70

Circle the better parent response.

Situation: The parents have agreed that their eight-year-old girl should be placed in a public school program for severely emotionally disturbed children. The parents are informed that psychotherapy for parents is required if the child is to remain in the program. They agree to this plan. The parents are expected to pay for this service on a private basis.

a. I have a concern about the costs involved.

b. I have a concern about the appropriateness of this placement.

LEAST-RESTRICTIVE ENVIRONMENT = Handicapped children should be educated with nonhandicapped children to the maximum extent possible.

This term does not mean that

- all children are to be educated in the regular classroom
- any particular setting (i.e., residential schools) will be abolished
- the child must spend the entire day in a regular classroom

EXERCISE 71

Circle the better response to the situation.

Situation: The local school district has no classes for blind children. It wants to place five-year-old Jimmy in the state school for the blind, a residential facility which is 200 miles from his home. The school district has always done this with blind children.

This is/is not an example of an attempt to implement the least-restrictive environmental concept.

a. is

b. is not

RELATED SERVICES = Developmental, corrective, and other supportive services as are required to assist the handicapped child. These include:

Speech pathology
Physical education
Psychological services
Physical and occupational therapy
Counseling services

EXERCISE 72

Circle the better response to the situation.

Situation: Johnny, who is a twleve-year-old learning disabled boy, is very clumsy and generally poorly coordinated. The gym teacher makes him sit on the sidelines when the boys play basketball and softball because he plays so badly.

Johnny is/is not receiving the services stipulated by law.

a. is

b. is not

Other supportive services include:

School health services
Transportation
Social work
Parent counseling and training

EXERCISE 73

Write a parent response which is related to the law.

Situation: The teacher and parent are having a telephone conversation.

Teacher: Your child has been misbehaving on the school bus and disturbing the other children. The principal says that the child may no longer ride the bus to and from school. You will have to arrange for your son's transportation yourself.

_____
_____
_____

EXERCISE 74

Circle the better response to the situation.

Situation: It is the spring of 1978. Special education services are now provided for handicapped individuals ages 5 to 18 by the State. The Federal Law says that all handicapped children between the ages of 3 and 21 must be included not later than September, 1980. The parents expect that Kelly, who has just turned 17 and has been labeled educably mentally impaired, will continue school until age 21. They are at a conference to plan the next year's program.

Counselor: Well, Kelly will be in the 1979 senior class next year. It will be her last year of high school.

The counselor's statement shows awareness/lack of awareness of the law.

a. awareness
b. lack of awareness

The school must contact parents about the possibility of their child being considered for special education services or placement. The parents should be provided with both written and oral notices of intent by the school to do any evaluation. Evaluation includes informal assessments, observations, or formal testing. The notice must be in the native language of the parent. The parents' written consent must be given before the evaluation process may begin.

EXERCISE 75

Circle the better response to the situation.

Situation: Mrs. Jones, who grew up in Kentucky, works as a housekeeper to support her family. She never went to school. One of her three children is having some difficulty keeping up academically with his classmates. His teacher sends Mrs. Jones a letter stating her concern for the boy and asking Mrs. Jones' permission to have the school psychologist test him. Mrs. Jones cannot read the letter and does not respond to the school. The teacher thinks Mrs. Jones is being uncooperative and sends her another letter notifying her that the psychological evaluation has taken place.

The school district is/is not following procedures prescribed by law.

a. is
b. is not

Every handicapped child must be fairly assessed so that there may be proper placement or service. States are to adopt procedures to insure that testing materials are appropriate and not racially or culturally biased and that testing take place in the language of the home.

EXERCISE 76

Rank the appropriateness of each of the following situations (1 = most appropriate, 3 = inappropriate).

Situation: An individual testing session is being conducted for a child who speaks Spanish as his primary language.

___ a. Tester: How are you?

___ b. Tester: Como esta usted?

___ c. Tester: How are you?
    Interpreter: Como esta usted?

The school is responsible for initiating and conducting meetings for the purpose of developing, reviewing, and revising the child's individualized program. The following procedures must be followed by the school to meet the minimum due process standards concerning such meetings:

   a. "good-faith" attempt to have parent at the meeting
   b. schedule meetings at a mutually agreed upon time and place
   c. notify the parent of the meeting early enough to insure attendance
   d. inform the parent as to the purpose, time, and location of the meeting
   e. inform the parent of all those who will attend the meeting

EXERCISE 77

Circle those requirements which have not been satisfied.

Situation: The special education teacher telephones the parent at 9:30 p.m.

Teacher: Hi, Mr. Phillips. There will be a 9 a.m. meeting tomorrow morning at the school, and we'll discuss Bill's program at that time. Can you come?

        a   b   c   d   e

The law identifies those who will decide on the child's placement and program. The participants at the meeting must include:

a. a representative of the local or regional school district who can provide or supervise services

b. the child's teacher

c. the parent(s)

d. the child where appropriate

e. other individuals at the discretion of the parent or agency

EXERCISE 78

Write a parent response which refers to the law.

Situation: The parent asks the principal if a friend may accompany him to the I.E.P. meeting.

Principal: No. I don't think so. There are too many people scheduled to be there already.

_____
_____
_____

Meetings to review and revise (if necessary) each child's individualized educational program should be held at least once per year.

EXERCISE 79

Write a statement which refers to the law.

Situation: Telephone conversation with parent.

Teacher: When you were out of town, I spoke with the psychologist, and we've reviewed Jimmy's tests. We've designed the I.E.P. for next year. We really worked on this, and I think you'll be delighted. When can you come in to sign it?

Parent: _____
_____
_____
_____

Parents have the right to complain or question evaluation procedures.

EXERCISE 80

Circle statements the parent might make.

Situation: Pat was tested by the school psychologist, who reports that the child seems to have regressed academically and needs placement in a lower-functioning group.

Parent: On the day you tested Pat, he returned home from school with a fever and a bad headache.

a. I feel that this testing session was unfair since Pat was not feeling well that day.

b. I'd like to know how well you'd do if someone tested you when you have a headache or fever.

c. I would like to have Pat retested on a day that he is feeling well.

The following factors are to be considered by the public agency when evaluation data are interpreted and placement decisions made:

  a. Several sources of information are used, including achievement and aptitude tests, observations, informal assessments, teacher recommendations, and background information.
  b. Several tests are used.
  c. Several persons, including those who know the child, participate in the placement decision.
  d. Least-restrictive alternatives are considered.

EXERCISE 81

Circle the factors that were not considered.

Situation: The psychologist is making recommendations to the mother at a planning conference.

Psychologist: This test shows a very disturbed child. He is severely depressed. I think he should be removed from his home immediately and placed in a residential treatment center. If not, one day you will find him with a noose around his neck.

        a   b   c   d

The law requires that a range of alternative educational placements be available to meet the needs of the handicapped shild. Instruction can therefore take place in a regular or special class or at home, hospital, special school, or institution. Supplemental services such as a resource room or itinerant instruction are to be provided if the child is in a regular education class and needs such services.

EXERCISE 82

Which situation fulfills the requirement of the legislation?

a. All twenty children who are labeled acoustically impaired spend the entire day in Mrs. Jones' class.

b. Some of the children who are labeled acoustically impaired are in special classes all day, some are in a resource room, and some are in the regular classroom.

The individualized educational program is a written statement for each child and must include:

    a. a statement of current level of performance
    b. a statement of annual goals and short-term instructional objectives
    c. criteria for evaluation
    d. evaluation procedures to determine if objectives are being achieved

EXERCISE 83

Circle the sections of the I.E.P. which are omitted.

Situation: The following is an excerpt from Debbie's I.E.P. "Debbie can now count objects through 10 with greater than 90% accuracy. She will now begin addition and subtraction through the number 5."

        a   b   c   d

Individualized plans must also include:

- the specific education services to be included (reading, math, etc.)
- the related services to be provided (speech therapy, physical therapy, transportation)
- the extent to which the child will participate in regular education programs (physical education, vocational education, music, art)

EXERCISE 84

Write a question the parent should ask.

Situation: During the planning meeting, speech therapy and music are mentioned as well as other education programs for Seth. When Mrs. Smith sees the written plan for her son, however, neither speech therapy nor music are mentioned.

___

___

___

If the parent (or agency) is dissatisfied with the results of the I.E.P. he/she may request an impartial hearing. Before the hearing the parent has the right to:

a. receive timely and specific notice of such a hearing

b. review and copy all records

c. obtain independent evaluations

d. be accompanied and advised by counsel and by individuals having special knowledge or training

EXERCISE 85

Match the parent statements with the right specified in parent rights listed above.

__ Mrs. Jones, I was given your name by the local parent organization as an advocate who might come to a hearing with me and advise me and help me plead my case.

__ I would like to make copies of all my child's reports.

__ Tomorrow we have an appointment at the Child Guidance Clinic, and Monday we're scheduled at the Speech Clinic for an evaluation.

Hearings are formal and complicated procedures. The parents have additional rights which include the right to:

a. confront and cross examine
b. bring witnesses and present evidence
c. receive a complete and accurate written and/or audio record of the proceedings.
d. appeal the decision

Because of the complexity of the procedure and the amount of preparation and degree of emotional investment which may be required, the parent should seriously consider seeking help from an attorney or advocate.

Section 504 of the Rehabilitation Act of 1973 is a basic civil rights provision which prohibits discrimination against handicapped individuals regardless of age or disability. The law states that qualified handicapped persons must be given the opportunity to benefit from programs or activities available to nonhandicapped individuals and that facilities housing the programs must be accessible to handicapped persons.

EXERCISE 86

Write a parent response which refers to the law.

Situation: Amanda's legs are paralyzed, and she uses a wheelchair. Amanda and her parents are requesting that she be transferred from the special orthopedic school she now attends to the regular high school near her home, the only high school in the district. There is general agreement at the meeting that Amanda would do well in this setting.

Principal of the high school: We'd love to have Amanda at our school, but there is no way that she can enter the building in her wheelchair.

_____
_____
_____

Section 504 also stipulates that academic adjustments and adaptations in the manner in which courses are conducted must be made to accommodate the needs of handicapped individuals.

EXERCISE 87

Write a response the student might make which refers to the law.

Situation: A blind student enrolls in an 11th grade American history course. He explains to the teacher that he would like to bring a tape recorder to class every day to facilitate his note taking. He also asks for special arrangements in order to take the weekly quizzes and exams. He needs to have someone read the questions to him, and instead of writing his answers he will use his typewriter to respond.

Teacher: I would really love to help you, but I'm feeling overwhelmed. The class is really too large for such individual requests. Perhaps you might take a different class which has fewer students.

_____
_____
_____

The law stipulates that when appropriate, the handicapped child himself should be included in the planning process. It is also a good idea for parents to encourage their handicapped children to be assertive on their own behalf.

According to the Family Rights and Privacy Act, parents have the following rights:

a. Parents of a student under 18 years of age must be permitted to inspect and review all records maintained by the school.
b. Parents must give written consent for the release or transfer of the records to someone outside the school system.
c. Only people who have a "legitimate educational interest" in the particular student may have access to the records.

EXERCISE 88

Circle those rights which have been violated.

Situation: A professor at the local university asks the school system for permission to investigate a number of student records for research he is conducting. The school gives permission.

                    a   b   c

Parents are also entitled to make additions to a report with which they disagree and to add their own viewpoint. A student over 18 years of age becomes entitled to see his own records and must give written consent for the release of his/her records.

EXERCISE 89

Circle the assertive parent response.

Situation: The following statement was written by a social worker in a report which was sent to the school.

"These parents are in great need of counseling. They have unrealistic expectations for their child. Most important, they need to improve their extremely negative behavior towards the professionals who are trying to help them."

a. The parent goes to the school and writes the following simple explanation which is added to the report: "We disagree with this point and would be willing to discuss our discipline and expectations with any school professional who is involved with our child."

b. The parent goes to the school and says the following to the principal: "You have no right to file a report with that kind of writing in it. Who do those people think they are?"

Parents may also make direct requests for change and are entitled to have sections deleted which they feel are unfair or untrue.

EXERCISE 90

Circle the assertive parent response.

Situation: The parents feel that the report written by the social worker in exercise 89 is unfair.

Parents to social worker

a. Ms. Sims, I've read your report, and I am upset by the section referring to our expectations. I feel it is unfair and would like that section removed from the report.

b. Ms. Sims, how could you possibly write that kind of biased and unfair report? I just can't understand you. Why don't you like us?

Parents have a right to privacy concerning their personal or family life. They are not required to discuss issues or opinions that do not directly relate to the educational programming of their child.

EXERCISE 91

Circle the assertive parent response.

Social worker: I understand that you're recently divorced and that now there is a man living in your house. Could you tell me who he is.

Mother:

a. Well, ugh, that's a friend of mine. I, well, his name is . . .

b. I don't think that topic is relevant to our discussion of John's academic program.

EXERCISE 92

Circle the assertive parent response.

Situation: The psychologist and parent are discussing two alternative placements for a mentally impaired child. One setting is more restrictive and designed for a more severely involved child.

Psychologist: Mr. Alvar, what do you see as the future for your son when he is an adult?

Parent response:

a. The way my child functions now should be the deciding factors in his placement.

b. Oh, I don't know. I worry about that all the time. I'm really not sure at this point in time.

Summary

The law exists to provide and protect the rights of handicapped individuals and their parents. However, parents need not always refer to the legislation during conferences. The parent should enter a conference talking about "my child" rather than "the law." The law should be referred to within the context of the question: What's best for my child?

The individual first learning about the law might think the following:
- The law is fixed and unchanging.
- The law contains an answer for every possible question.
- One merely refers to the law when a question arises.

These statements, however, are not accurate. The law cannot always be read and easily interpreted. Lawyers would be unnecessary if this were true. The law is open to interpretation. Rarely, if ever, can school personnel say:
- The law says we must do this.
- The law says we cannot do this.

There are always ways of using the law to support one's point of view. Often the parent will become aware that in one city the school system works in one way within the law and that in a nearby city the law is used legally in quite an opposite manner.

As parents begin to work with the law they find that interpretations are constantly in flux. They will find that the law

(1) is not always clearly written;

(2) will be amended;

(3) is used by different people in different ways.

Laws are often ignored and unenforced until a lawsuit forces their implementation. Parents must remember that the law exists and its intent will be realized only if it is implemented.

In attempting to understand the various laws governing the education of handicapped children, parents will do well to turn to parent organizations in their town or city. These organizations, and their attorneys, can usually be of assistance in interpreting the law as it relates to specific situations and in helping parents find possible solutions to legal problems. Again, parents must remember that the primary focus of the conference is the child, not the law. The law exists to provide and protect rights, but it is not always necessary to rely on the law or refer to legislation in order to do so.

PART VI. PROBLEMS AND STRATEGIES

Introduction

Whether their child is handicapped or not, all parents are involved in a long set of interactions with persons bearing responsibility for their child's education. Parents are constantly encountering personnel who represent various medical, social, and educational agencies which have the capacity to provide necessary services. During these interactions:

- There will be problems, conflicts, and tensions, some not always avoidable or unnecessary.
- There will be gaps and lags in the time required for both parents and educators to learn and understand legislative mandates and to accommodate new attitudes and approaches within their decision-making process.
- There will be both positive and negative interactions — some in which the parent will feel successful and some in which the parent will feel despondent and frustrated.

The expectation and management of problems and conflicts are an integral part of the long-term process involved in attempting to plan and evaluate for a handicapped child.

The intent of the legislation for parent involvement in the decision-making process will require for its implementation some changes in both the attitudes and skills of many professionals, and parents need to be aware of discrepancies between the professional's expectation of the parent role and that prescribed by the legislation. If, for example, the teacher feels that the main function of the parent is generally to give and provide information rather than specifically to review progress or make final decisions, the likelihood is great that assertive behavior, regardless of how skillfully executed, will be perceived as inappropriate and possibly aggressive. To avoid unnecessary conflict and to plan productive strategies the parent might ask questions to identify the attitudes of school personnel relative to parent involvement.

EXERCISE 93

Circle the question(s) which could be asked by a parent to clarify expectations.

a. What do you think is my role here today?

b. Who do you feel makes the final decision?

Parents who bring a tape recorder to a conference, requesting permission to record the meeting (perhaps for the absent spouse), report fewer digressions and problems and more helpful behaviors on the part of school personnel.

Conflict

Conflict does and will occur. It should, in fact, be expected. Conflict is a consequence of differing values and opinions, shortages of resources, ignorance, and misunderstandings. The goal cannot be to avoid conflict at any cost but to negotiate and resolve it whenever possible. Conflict is an important element in communication, and its effective resolution may be one of the critical differences between "good" and "bad" relationships.

EXERCISE 94

Circle the parent statements concerning conflicts which set a positive tone.

a. Well, it looks as though this is one of those difficult situations we anticipated. It will be difficult and really require our energy to resolve.

b. I knew that some day you'd turn on me.

c. We may not see eye to eye on this issue, but there will be other times when we'll agree.

Minor conflicts too frequently and needlessly develop into major problems. The battle lines are drawn, and the adversaries view themselves and each other in terms of winning and losing. Such feelings too often center on the interactions of adults rather than on the needs of children.

EXERCISE 95

Circle the parent statement which best attempts to avoid unnecessary conflict.

a. You're mistaken if you think you can dictate to me.

b. Let's keep in mind that we're here to plan for Barbara's program.

c. I think this problem requires some compromise for each one of us.

d. The issue I raised isn't that important and seems to be confusing the situation. I can bring it up at another time.

Constant avoidance of important or troublesome issues, however, tends to increase and complicate problems. Parents and school personnel must deal with issues, face problems, and learn to cope and manage unpleasant situations.

EXERCISE 96

Circle the parent statement which shows a willingness to deal with a delicate issue.

Situation: An 8-year-old brain-injured child undressed in class twice in the past week.

a. What are you saying about my child?

b. This type of behavior is upsetting, but we'll have to talk about it.

EXERCISE 97

> Situation: Frank is hearing impaired and is completing his third year in school. He was mainstreamed for half the day. Although reports have stated that Frank is capable, he is not doing well in reading. The parent knows of other programs in reading that have proved effective with some children.
>
> Parent:
>
> a. I know that you have tried to set up an effective reading program, but I just don't see the progress we all hoped for. I think we might try a different approach.
>
> b. Well, at least Frank is certainly doing very well in his social interactions with the children. He's happy in the classroom.

Strategies should be utilized which help to negotiate differences rather than to ignore or stifle them. Resolution of conflict should not be a win-lose situation but a compromise in which the most positive results for all the parties are negotiated and agreed upon. Solutions or attempts at resolution should be seen as coping and competent responses to problems. It is often helpful for group members to answer a series of questions relative to defining and solving a problem. The process can be an effective and systematic procedure for attempting to resolve conflicts. It is often best to begin with those topics around which there is agreement among the group and progress from there to the areas of least disagreement, saving the main disagreement for last. Conflict resolution involves a three step procedure.

1. Defining the Conflict or Problem

    a. What is the problem?

    b. What are the factors which influence the problem?

    c. What are areas of agreement, minor disagreement, and major disagreement?

EXERCISE 98

> *Match the parent statements with the questions listed at the bottom of the preceding page.*
>
> _ There seems to be an attitude that he doesn't need to improve his skills.
>
> _ I feel that there is a problem concerning David's arithmetic.
>
> _ It sounds as though we all feel that he can recognize numbers and count from one to twenty.

2. <u>Selecting a Solution</u>

    a. What solutions are proposed?
    b. How are the solutions ranked and which ones are high priority?
    c. What would indicate that a reasonable degree of success has been attained?

EXERCISE 99

> *Match the statements with the questions listed above.*
>
> _ Consultant: I know of some new materials.
>
> _ Teacher: The most important thing is having an aide.
>
> _ Parent: I feel that David needs a lot of practice. Perhaps he needs an aide.
>
> _ I would feel that David had progressed if he could purchase candy at the shops using simple addition and subtraction.

3. <u>Establishing a Plan</u>

    a. What action should be taken?
    b. Who is responsible?
    c. When will action be initiated and reviewed?

EXERCISE 100

Match the statements with the questions listed at the bottom of the preceding page.

___ Let's try out the materials for one week, and if they look promising we'll begin with the aide on 11/1. Let's talk about this the week of 12/6.

___ Consultant: Since I'm so familiar with the materials, I'd like to test them out with David.

___ Perhaps we can try out the materials with David, and if they're useful the aides could use them during the daily math time.

Some concerns or conflicts about mainstreaming which have been identified by parents include:

- Will the regular classroom teacher want my child in her class?
- Will the regular classroom teacher know how to teach my child?
- Will the other children accept my child as a friend?
- Will my child feel good about himself if he is in a regular class?
- Will he learn more or less in the regular class?

List some of your own questions, concerns or problems.

_____
_____
_____
_____
_____
_____

It may be helpful to practice answering questions about your own problem or conflict. Use the worksheet on the next page.

WORKSHEET: CONFLICT RESOLUTION

Defining the Problem:

    a. What is the problem?

    b. What are the factors which influence the problem (e.g., attitudes, cost)?

    c. What are areas of agreement, minor disagreement, and major disagreement?

Generating Solutions:

    d. What solutions can be proposed?

    e. How would the solutions be ranked in priority?

    f. What would indicate that a reasonable degree of success has been attained?

Establishing a Plan:

    g. What action should be taken?

    h. Who should be responsible for the action?

    i. Whan would action be instructed and reviewed?

WORKSHEET: CONFLICT RESOLUTION

Use this worksheet to note the effectiveness of your plan.

Results of the Plan:

    Positive

    Negative

Reasons for the Results:

Satisfaction with the Results:

Ideas for the Future:

Engaging in these activities may provide information, clarify positions, or generate new strategies. The sequence just described attempts to develop a systematic analysis and decision-making process. It hinges on some measure of negotiation between those responsible for providing services and the consumers for whom the law was designed; it tries to avoid a power struggle between adversaries – there is some win for everybody. The process may fail, of course, but it is a point of departure. The steps to take involve some confrontation around the disagreement, negotiation, and then compromise towards resolution. Unfortunately, those at school conferences may not be able to negotiate and resolve all conflicts. It is apparent that:

- Some issues will be resolved unfairly for someone.
- Some people feel that they must always win.
- Parents sometimes don't know what's best for their children
- Some educators don't like children.
- All people have pressures upon them, sometimes unrelated to the task at hand, that cause them to act in unproductive ways.

When informal conflict-resolution strategies fail, parents may have to assert themselves and use more formal procedures, such as hearings and complaint procedures. However, such procedures are usually emotionally charged, technical in nature and extremely time consuming. Therefore, parents considering such actions should contact other parents (or parent groups) who have experience in these areas. They can best provide current information on the potential benefits and/or problems of formal actions. Although parents may not be accustomed to using these strategies and may feel guilty when doing so, the choice may be unavoidable. Sometimes the mere idea of this kind of action may prompt school personnel to consider alternatives not previously considered.

EXERCISE 101

Circle the more assertive parent response.

Principal: If we can't resolve this issue, we will be forced into a hearing.

Parent:

a. Oh, that's such a formal procedure. Perhaps we can think things over again.
b. All right. I feel that I've attempted to negotiate, but since I see no solutions in sight, I guess a hearing is appropriate.

Concerns relative to school reports can be a potential source of conflict, the resolution of which may require the parent to ask difficult questions or make direct requests. Written reports might reflect disagreements and discrepancies in attitudes and information between professionals and between professionals and parents and result in parents receiving double messages about their child's capacities and progress or their own behaviors. For example, in order to move a child into another class, the teacher may write a glowing and positive report even though it inaccurately describes the child's classroom behavior.

Sometimes professionals hedge in the terms they use to describe a child. They may say the child is "slow" rather than retarded because they don't want to "worry" the parent. Reports like these can engender false expectations on the parents' part and lead to confusion and frustration. Parents are especially confused when they receive conflicting reports from professionals.

EXERCISE 102

Circle the assertive parent's question.

Situation: The parent is sent a report from a psychologist which labels the child as a "loner," and "isolate"; however, the teacher's yearly evaluation states: "Johnny is doing quite well socially."

a. How do you explain the discrepancy between these two reports?

b. Someone's lying. What's going on?

On the other hand, some school reports may be written in anger, anger at a disrupting child or a disturbing parent. Too often, when parents do stand up for their rights, question procedures, or disagree with professionals, they make the professionals angry. The professionals may then vent their anger in negative reports written to the school. Parents can avoid or prevent such situations by requesting to review every final report written by a professional before it is forwarded to an agency or school. If the parents feel that the report is inappropriate or unfair they should not give their permission for its release.

EXERCISE 103

> *Circle the better parent response.*
>
> Situation: The report has been completed and reviewed by the clinical supervisor in a hospital.
>
> Supervisor: Mr. Johnson, we've completed the evaluation of your son William. We've included the assessments and recommendation we previously discussed, and they will be sent to the school this week.
>
> Parent:
> a. Thank you very much. I hope that the recommendation concerning physical education was included.
> b. I would like to review the report before it is sent to the school.

Self Management of Tension and Anxiety

Parents may feel tense or angry during a conference. It is possible, however, for them to develop skills to cope with the tension and anger brought on by the inevitable conflicts that arise. Sometimes the mere thought of friction initiates in parents a series of negative behaviors which impede productive coping. The strategies that can be used to cope with tension include the following:

1. Be aware of tension. The parent should look for signals of sudden, rising or unwanted tension by gaining information from:

    - one's self: set up a simple system which requires you to rate or describe your feeling(s) or tension level at 10-20 minute intervals throughout the conference.
    - others: prior to the conference, arrange for an advocate, friend, or spouse to be present at the meeting and to signal if you show undesired signs of tension.

2. Manage the tension. Once aware of undesired tension, the parent should actively engage in behaviors which will contain or reduce the anxiety. Anxiety-management strategies involving physical or mental behaviors should be identified, discussed, and practiced prior to the conference. Ways of coping with tension might include:

    - physical behaviors:
        a. Take several deep breaths and try to relax.
        b. Tense and relax some muscles of the body (arms, legs).
        c. Stand up and stretch or move for a minute.

d. Ask for a 1-2 minute break and walk around the room.

   e. Look at a friend, advocate, or spouse who looks relaxed and attempt to model his/her behavior.

   f. Shift attention to some physical activity for a moment, i.e., have a cigarette, piece of candy, cup of coffee, write notes.

- mental behaviors

   a. Give yourself positive messages such as, "Relax now. I will breathe deeply for a minute or two and feel my tense muscles relax."

   "Relax. I can control my feelings."

   "Yes, I have been coping thus far and can continue."

   b. Imagine youself as calm and competent. This could include seeing yourself efficiently manage or perform in the conference or other situations.

EXERCISE 104

Circle the behaviors or statements which might help the parent effectively manage her feelings.

Situation: The parent of a preschool child is at the I.E.P. meeting.

Teacher statement: Look, Mrs. Wagner, I don't see why you won't agree to the child attending school for just one hour a day. You're just trying to get rid of George by insisting that he stay for a full morning session. We're not baby sitters.

a. Excuse me. I think I'll get a drink at the water fountain.

b. Who are you to talk to me that way.

c. Bang a fist on the table and walk out.

d. Think to self: I'd better take a deep breath and relax.

e. Think to self: If I could manage myself with the psychologist last week, I can maintain control now.

f. Open and close fists, expanding, and contracting the muscles of the arm.

Parents should identify the emotions they feel — whether anger, fear, pleasure, or perplexity.

EXERCISE 105

Circle words which describe the emotions the mother might have.

Situation: The psychologist makes the following recommendation at a planning and placement conference: These tests show a very disturbed child. He is severely depressed. I think he needs to be removed from his home immediately and placed in a residential treatment center. If not, one day you will find him with a noose around his neck.

a. shock
b. anger
c. pleasure
d. concern

EXERCISE 106

Circle the assertive parent response which describes the mother's feelings.

a. That type of statement is shocking to a parent.
b. I just can't believe what you're saying. You're wrong.

It is not uncommon to experience feelings of uneasiness when confronting strangers and/or the prospect of conflict, which is often unavoidable. Parents may find it productive to provide a brief, honest, and direct statement that shares these feelings with others.

EXERCISE 107

> What could you say to the teacher to share your feelings?
>
> Situation: You are on your way to the conference room where you will work with the teacher. Your stomach is quivering and your palms sweating.
>
> _____
> _____
> _____
> _____

Remember a recent school conference or discuss a meeting with a friend. List the different emotions, fears or anxieties that you had.

_____
_____
_____

List activities you engaged in to deal with your emotions or manage the tension.

_____
_____
_____

Being aware of their rights does not automatically guarantee that parents will stand up for them. Parents may have anxieties and fears about the consequences of assertive behavior which may inhibit their willingness to act assertively. The statements that parents say to themselves can reduce anxiety and support their attempts to act more assertively when necessary.

EXERCISE 108

Circle the statements which would support assertive parent behavior.

1. If I stand up for my rights then:
   a. School personnel will be angry with me. They won't like me.
   b. The results may be positive, neutral, or negative. I have legitimate rights and I have a choice. Besides, school people may not like me even if I don't stand up for my rights.
2. If I act in an assertive manner and school officials do become angry then:
   a. It will be horrible. I will be devastated.
   b. It's their problem. I will try to manage the situation.
3. If I am honest or disagree with the teacher, whom I like then:
   a. We may interact in a more effective manner.
   b. I will hurt her feelings.
4. If I refuse a legitimate request from a teacher or principal then:
   a. People will think I am irresponsible and impossible to deal with.
   b. People will have to realize that even legitimate requests may be turned down if I feel that there is a better alternative for my child.
5. If I am not an expert but do have an opinion, question, or concern, then:
   a. I should express myself even though I might lack information or make a mistake. It's all right not to be perfect.
   b. I must avoid making mistakes or asking questions. I might look ignorant or stupid.

EXERCISE 109

Write a productive parent self-statement.

Situation: The teacher has just rejected a suggestion of the parent. The parent is very uncomfortable since he realizes that there is a conflict between the teacher and himself.

Parent self-statement:
_____
_____
_____
_____

The parent needs first to identify feelings and reactions and second to decide on the type of action to pursue.

EXERCISE 110

Complete a through d based on the following situation.

Situation: The conference is coming to a close. The parent is not satisfied with the proposed program.

Principal's statement: Well now, looks as though everything is all set. Right, Mrs. More?

a) Circle the feelings you might experience.

fear	defeat	anger	other
disappointment	happiness	tension	

b) Circle the assertive and productive behaviors you should engage in.

laugh	cry	yell
state feelings		state plans

c) Write a way you would manage tension.

_____

d) Write a response that describes your feelings and one that provides a suggestion for action.

feeling statement: _____

_____

action statement: _____

_____

EXERCISE 111

Complete a through e on the following situation.

Situation: The child is six years old and severely retarded. The parents feel very strongly that the child should live at home with the family and attend the public school. The child is not currently attending school. The conference is ending.

Principal: I'm a father of four children, and I really understand your concerns. What can I do? We just don't have a program with the kinds of services Johnny needs. He is so young and so severely handicapped. We'd need a teacher and an aide just for him. He's better off in a private or state facility.

a) Circle the feelings you might experience.

    fear   anger   disappointment   relief   defeat

    tension   other

b) Circle the action you would want to pursue.

    continue the conference   leave the conference

    set up another conference

c) Write ways you might manage tension.

d) Write a response that describes your feelings.

e) Write a response that refers to the law.

Repeated Assertion

It is often necessary to repeat a message in several ways. The parent need not refute, justify, or question the other person(s). The message to be communicated is merely repeated in a calm and firm manner. Valid points may be incorporated, but non-topic issues and argumentative words should not be mentioned.

EXERCISE 112

Circle the response which reflects repeated assertion.

Situation: A recommendation has been made for a psychiatric evaluation. The parent wants to wait and talk to the family physician.

Social worker: We've all suggested reasons why it would be more convenient for you to sign the consent form today.

Parent response:

a. I don't understand the reasons for this recommendation.

b. I have already explained several times the reason I will not be able to sign the form today.

EXERCISE 113

Situation: A child's placement hinges on several tests and observations conducted during a period of confusion and disruption in the family. The father wants additional assessments conducted.

Parent statement: I understand that an evaluation was conducted several months ago, but I'd like a second opinion since we had problems with the family at that time — things are better now.

Psychologist: This was a well-done evaluation. I am a certified psychologist doing this work for ten years. I don't think additional assessments are necessary.

Parent: I realize you feel you have done the right thing, but I'd still like a second evaluation.

Teacher: I still can't see why you want to subject the child to another evaluation.

Parent (statement of intent):
_____
_____
_____

Timing

The success of interactions between parents and school personnel may frequently depend on "timing." The time selected by the parent to react, ignore, initiate, or conclude action may well influence an entire sequence of events. Appropriate timing is frequently the deciding factor in the successful use of assertive skills. There are times when a parent may know how to react to extremely aggravating or provocative statements but decide against using assertive skills at that particular time. The parent judges that the only productive response is to ignore or pass over such statements and perhaps not return to the problem area. The parent's judgement of the situation will dictate his/her action. Assertive skills are in the parent's repertoire, but they are to be used when and if the parent decides that such behavior assists in the attainment of goals.

EXERCISE 114

Circle the appropriate parent statement.

Situation: The conference will end in a few minutes. The principal has made an extremely critical and negative remark. The parent does not care to deal with the remark at this time since an important issue is being discussed.

Parent:

a. Let's stick to the topic during the remaining few minutes.
b. I find your remarks insulting. That statement should be retracted.

Another aspect of timing involves sharing feelings or questioning a professional's judgement at the time an incident occurs or an issue is discussed. A well-timed reponse can avoid major confrontations or outbursts which are counterproductive.

EXERCISE 115

Circle the more assertive parent response.

Situation: Mrs. Parsons, Susie always looks so sloppy. Can't you do something with her appearance. Her hair's a mess, and her blouse is always hanging out of her skirt.

Parent:
a. That kind of statement makes me feel badly because it implies that I don't take care of my child.
b. Well, I guess I can try harder (the parent is thinking — Oh, the teacher thinks I don't care enough — that really makes me angry.)

EXERCISE 116

Circle questions or statements that are appropriate at this time.

Situation: A social worker has presented the results of some classroom observations and is suggesting program changes. The parent doesn't understand the total meaning of the results and doesn't like the suggestions being made.

a. You have a lot of experience....
b. I appreciate your skill and concern, but I really don't either fully understand or agree with your conclusions.

Time is also an important aspect of the law. For example, if parents do not act within the time limits prescribed by law they will lose their right to appeal. Professionals are required by law to provide such information to parents.

EXERCISE 117

Circle the appropriate responses.

Situation: The I.E.P. meeting has concluded, and Mrs. Pope, Susie's mother, is unhappy with the results. She decides to try to persuade the Director of Special Education to change his mind.

Instead of signing the form requesting a hearing (which in the State of Michigan must be signed within seven days) she says, "A hearing sounds so formal and legalistic. I don't want to make any trouble for anyone. Maybe I can persuade the Director of Special Education to change his mind."

a. The parent's timing   is / is not   appropriate.
b. If she is unhappy with the I.E.P., she should   sign / not sign   the form requesting a hearing.

Parents should ask professionals to state rules regarding the timing of procedures (i.e. referrals, complaints, hearings, appeals).

The idea of timing may include occasions when the parent cannot react or decide. Additional time may be necessary if there is a lot of information to consider and important decisions to be made. However, this should be requested <u>before the conclusion of the I.E.P.</u> Even if no additional time is requested, parents should verify time limits before the end of the meeting.

EXERCISE 118

Circle the more appropriate parent response.

Situation: The final decision on a preschool placement is to be made. Test results, medical reports, and alternatives have been discussed. The parent has been in the conference for two hours.

Director of Special Education: At this point we should be able to decide on a placement for Sally and conclude the I.E.P.

Parent:
a. This is an important decision. I feel I need some more time to consider all we've discussed today. I would like to request a recess of this I.E.P. until next week so that I can make my decision.
b. This is an important decision. We have talked about a lot of things. I'm not sure what to do but I guess we have to make a decision.

A good sense of timing can involve silence. Silence following an aggravating or provocative statement may underscore the inappropriateness of the statement, especially if the silence is accompanied by a direct gaze at the speaker. In fact, another participant may, without any encouragement, come to the parents' defense and protect the parents' interest.

EXERCISE 119

Circle the more appropriate parent response.

Situation: The speech pathologist interrupts the parent. The teacher says, "You're interrupting Mrs. Gabel. She's the parent, let her finish her remarks." The parent says, "You shouldn't interrupt me like that."

a. The parent's right   was / was not   being protected by the teacher.
b. The parent   should / should not   be silent at this time.

A strategy involved with timing involves the parents remaining silent and encouraging the professionals to discuss things among themselves. This is appropriate as long as the parents' views are being represented.

EXERCISE 120

Circle the appropriate response to the situation.

Situation: The teacher has suggested a plan involving the termination of services for a teenager. The parent is violently opposed to this plan. She thinks that Bill should receive further training.

Special education teacher: In summary, I feel that Bill should graduate now.

Vocational education counselor: Let me explain why I feel Bill would benefit from additional training. He should not graduate now.

a. The parent's views   are / are not   represented.

b. The parent needs / needs not   become involved at this time.

Sometimes the time for an appropriate parent response or reaction is missed. The parent may have reacted too slowly. By the time the parent's thoughts are organized the conversation has shifted to another subject. Several actions can be taken by parents who feel that the appropriate time to say something has passed. They may:

- write notes to themselves about the incident;
- take a break and discuss the matter with a friend, advocate, or spouse;
- bring the incident up at another time during or after the conference, expressing feelings about a particular statement;
- plan in advance for the next conference;
- practice making statements prior to the next conference;
- write a letter to the speaker after the conference expressing feelings about a particular statement.

EXERCISE 121

Circle the appropriate parent statement.

Situation: The principal made several questionable remarks about the parent during the conference. The parent is talking to the principal later that day.

Parent to principal:

a. It's difficult to understand the things people sometimes say during the conference.
b. Something you said during the conference bothered me. I'd like to discuss it with you.

Generating Assertive Responses

Becoming assertive involves not only distinguishing the differences among assertive, nonassertive, and aggressive behaviors but also attempting to produce one's own assertive responses. The parent has a variety of possible verbal responses from which to select. These may include direct open and honest statements of:

a. an opinion
b. a feeling
c. a legitimate right

EXERCISE 122

Read the description of the situation and rank each of the parent responses (a = opinion, b = feeling, c = right).

Situation: The principal, who is chairing the placement conference, says, "Your daughter's diagnostic workup indicates a moderate to severe learning disability, and we've decided that a special class placement is best. Please sign the consent form."

Parent response:

__ According to the state code, the diagnostic information should be available for me to examine.

__ I completely disagree with your recommendation.

__ I feel uncomfortable having to decide and sign the consent form right now.

During verbal interactions the parent may also:
- a. make a direct request
- b. deny a request
- c. ask a question

EXERCISE 123

Rank the following parent responses (a, b, c).

___ I will not sign the form at this time.

___ How do you explain the term "learning disabilities"?

___ I would like a further explanation of the program and a discussion of other options.

Additional possibilities are available to the parent. It may be appropriate for the parent to:

- a. confront or point out discrepancies
- b. persuade others
- c. empathize or understand the feelings of others

EXERCISE 124

Rank the following parent responses (a, b, c).

___ I think you should reconsider your suggestion for the following three reasons.

___ These procedures seem to differ from the ones used last year.

___ I understand your concern for this problem.

EXERCISE 125

Read each situation and write one or two possible assertive responses.

Right/problem: You are entitled to know about available services and to help decide if they should be used.

Situation: A reading consultant has completed testing and is speaking to the parent.

Consultant's statement: Your son's test show some problem areas, but at his age this is common. Give him time; he'll grow out of it.

Possible parent responses:
_____
_____
_____

EXERCISE 126

Right/problem: The parent has a right to help select an appropriate or feasible time to discuss the child.

Situation: The time is after school when the parent is picking up the child.

Teacher statement: Do you have a moment, Mrs. Wall? I'd like to talk to you about Jane.

Possible parent responses:
_____
_____
_____

EXERCISE 127

Right/problem: The parent is made to feel guilty. The parent has the right to participate/negotiate for the service.

Situation: A placement conference for a 5 and 1/2 year-old child.

Teacher statement: I don't see why you won't agree to the child attending school for just one hour a day. You're just trying to get rid of George by insisting that he stay for the full morning session. We're not baby sitters.

Possible parent responses:
_____
_____

It is difficult not to respond aggressively to the situation described in Exercise 127. The teacher's remark is a critical and blaming statement. The parent, in electing to act assertively rather than aggressively, decides to control the situation rather than be controlled by it. Losing one's temper and attacking the teacher only reinforces the stereotype of the "emotional parent." The parent could respond by saying, "That is a very provocative remark, but I won't deal with it at this time."

It is important for parents to communicate that they understand the feelings of the school personnel with whom they interact. Phrases such as, "I understand your feelings . . ." or "Your concern is appreciated . . ." show empathy and indicate respect and consideration for others but do not infer deference. The parent may combine empathetic statements with statements that directly express his/her concerns.

EXERCISE 128

Circle the empathetic parent response.

Teacher: I really feel it would be best for Barbara to go to the regular classrooms in the morning.

Parent:

a. Barbara and I have discussed this issue during the past two weeks. Both of us feel that this is not something to do at this time.
b. I understand that you want Barbara to interact with nonspecial education students, but I don't feel she will benefit from this type of experience at this time.

When initiating statements or responding to others, the parent may make statements which express a:

       a. concern
       b. compliment
       c. humorous remark
       d. empathy and understanding

EXERCISE 129

Write in the letter, a, b, c, or d, which describes each part of the parent's statement.

Situation: Susie is in a residential facility which the parents basically like very much. However, during the last few months the child's academic achievements have noticeably declined.

Parent statement:

__ St. Clair's School has a really fine and supportive program.

__ I understand and appreciate that the teachers spend a great deal of time with the children.

__ I have become concerned recently about the decrease in Susie's reading and writing skills that I have noticed.

EXERCISE 130

Write an assertive statement for the situation in Exercise 129.

_____

_____

_____

EXERCISE 131

Situation: You have just presented your suggestions to those at the conference: the principal, teacher, and psychologist. It is obvious that the psychologist does not agree with you.

Psychologist statement: Your suggestions don't seem workable. Your plans lack an indepth perspective and sensitivity to the dynamics of this complex situation.

Your response: _____

_____

_____

EXERCISE 132

> Situation: You and the teacher are discussing your child. The conversation continues to center only on the negative aspects of his behavior. You want to suggest that the teacher identify and plan around some positive attributes of your child.
>
> Teacher statement: In addition, Billy is always yelling.
>
> Your response: _____
> _____
> _____

Nonassertion

Assertiveness is a skill used by parents to help them obtain the best possible school program for their child. Parents who act assertively affirm their rights in interaction with shool personnel. But sometimes affirming rights and obtaining the best possible school program for the child may become conflicting goals. Parents must always remember that the major goal is the child's school program.

As we have stated previously, sometimes schools see themselves as institutions dispensing charity. In return, they expect the recipient (the parents) to be grateful – not assertive. At other times, although school personnel agree that a good school program is the child's legitimate right, they do not want the parents to participate as equals in the planning of the program. In this case, assertive behavior on the part of the parent may be perceived as inappropriate or aggressive.

Some professionals, because of their own personality factors, want to control the parent and the child. Indeed, they chose their profession because of their need to be in control and to feel powerful. In this case, a parent who is assertive would be extremely threatening to them.

In all these situations, it is perfectly possible for the schools and their personnel to provide excellent educational programs for the handicapped children they serve, even while violating many of the parents' basic human rights. The parents must always keep in mind their major goal: the welfare of the child.

Example

Fourteen-year-old Joan is attending a special six-week summer camp run by the school system for retarded children. The director of the summer program, who is also an elementary school principal, is known as "the Admiral." She runs an excellent program, and Joan's parents feel that their daughter is benefiting from it a great deal. However, the director, an extremely controlling person, often treats the parents quite disrespectfully and inhumanely. The parents, in turn, are often angry at her. However, the parents attempt to ignore the director's behavior toward them as adults and to pay attention to the excellent services she provides to their children.

Think of a future conference or discuss an upcoming meeting with a friend. List issued (and/or personnel) for which assertive behavior would be appropriate.

_____
_____
_____
_____
_____

Summary

Parents will encounter problems and conflicts during interactions with school personnel. The problems will differ according to the type or severity of the handicap and the age and sex of the child, the individuals or schools involved and other situations (i.e., budgetary restraint) which exist in the community at a particular time.

However, regardless of the uniqueness of their problems, parents must have a set of strategies ready to cope with the unpleasantries, uncertainties and conflicts that inevitably occur.

Systematic procedures for resolving conflict, affirming rights, coping with tension, and managing anxiety have been suggested. In addition, appropriate timing has been described as a critical aspect in the successful use of such strategies.

Therefore, although problems often seem overwhelming and insolvable, techniques do exist which enable parents to analyze, cope, and work towards resolutions. The use of such skills allows parents to view themselves as problem solvers. They enter conferences with confidence rather than apprehension, feel in control and can contribute to the educational planning process.

PART VII. SKILL DEVELOPMENT

Introduction

Awareness of one's rights and identification of appropriate or inappropriate behaviors are but one step towards more effective communication and interaction with school personnel. Because assertive responses may be newly acquired behaviors and often must be integrated into a larger pattern of behaviors, the parent, as any new learner, usually requires preparation and practice. The parent should therefore experiment with newly learned verbal and nonverbal assertive behaviors and rehearse situations which might be encountered in the future or which have previously been difficult to manage. In addition, the parent must systematically prepare for conferences during which he/she and school personnel will decide on the child's placements and program options.

Modeling

The modeling of appropriate behaviors is a critical aspect in improving assertive or general personal-effectiveness skills. A model can provide an entire behavioral picture of a complex set of skills. The subtle aspects of both verbal and nonverbal behaviors can be observed, imitated, and practiced after observing a model.

It is adviseable, therefore, to engage in interactions/practice sessions with those who are experienced and can provide models of positive and effective behaviors involving parents and school personnel. Specific on-task features of the model's behavior should be described and discussed before, during, and after a demonstration.

Behavioral Rehearsal

The purpose of a behavioral rehearsal is to explore, develop, and practice assertive conference behaviors in a safe environment. Such practice increases the parent's awareness of his/her own productive and nonproductive behaviors. Skills requiring timing and spontaneity, which are difficult to perfect during an actual conference, may be repeated and improved in a low-risk situation.

Lastly, a discussion following a behavioral rehearsal can provide the parent with useful feedback and support. Positive feedback should be provided concerning each task-oriented verbal and nonverbal behavior. Criticism and confrontation are usually avoided.

Situations

Read the following situations which could be used for a behavioral rehearsal:

1. You want your child to be placed in a regular kindergarten. He tests in the high educable mentally retarded range. John is six years old and well adjusted. You think he would benefit from being with "normal" children. However, the school wants to place him in a special class for educable mentally retarded children.
2. Your child is in the sixth grade, small for his age, reads at the fourth-grade level and is quite immature. The school wants to promote him to the seventh grade at the local junior high school. You feel he should be retained in the sixth grade and given extra help with his academic and social skills.
3. Your son is not progressing in reading. You have discussed this with the teacher who assures you that he's doing fine. During the summer, you have reviewed many reading materials and have prepared a sequence of activities you feel is good. You are presenting it at the conference and requesting that it be used.
4. Previous testing sessions have been a disaster. Your child is usually terrified and resists interacting with strangers. You have found some strategies that seem successful. You want to inform the psychologist of the problem and discuss methods of keeping your daughter calm.

Worksheet: Behavioral Rehearsal

Describe a situation you might like to rehearse:

Background or problem:

Participants: (i.e., teacher, psychologist, principal, others)

Location:

Time:

Topics to be discussed:

Questions to be asked:

Outcome(s) you desire:

Ranking Systems for Behavioral Rehearsal

Several types of ranking systems may be used while observing a behavioral rehearsal. They vary according to the degree of information or feedback provided to the participant.

A ranking system, which can be used early in training, provides an overall judgement of behavior. Such a system might be used when scenes are to be enacted only once or as a stimulus for discussion. Each category of behavior (i.e., verbal, nonverbal) would be ranked using the following symbols:

− = aggressive,   0 = nonassertive,   + = assertive

A ranking system which provides a greater degree of variation for each behavior contains a multi-point scale. This ranking system may be used when individuals want to rehearse a scene several times in order to improve their performance. Each behavior of a participant would be ranked using the following scale system:

-3	-2	-1	0	+1	+2	+3
aggressive			passive			assertive

A ranking system designed for group discussion and feedback uses the following scoring guidelines:

1 = Very poor
2 = Fair
3 = Average
4 = Good
5 = Excellent

Whenever possible, a model (parent, advocate, mental health professional) should model the appropriate behaviors required in the situation to be rehearsed.

Observation Form: Behavioral Rehearsal

The parent should practice and rehearse assertive behaviors prior to conferences. This rehearsal is best done with other persons, such as spouses, friends, or parents. If necessary, the parent can practice such behaviors periodically using a tape recorder.

Rehearse a scene and have someone observe and rank each person's behavior, using the rankings below. (Individuals who rehearse a scene should rank themselves afterwards.)

| | Person #1 | Person #2 |
	name	name
Verbal Behaviors		
Loudness	_____	_____
Speed	_____	_____
Pitch	_____	_____
Content or message	_____	_____

Comments:

Nonverbal Behaviors
Eye contact	_____	_____
Body position/posture	_____	_____
Body movement	_____	_____
Facial expression	_____	_____
Gestures	_____	_____

Comments:

Discussion Guide: Behavioral Rehearsal

Answer the following questions about each person:
1. What degree of consistency existed between the message and the manner in which the words were delivered?
2. What degree of consistency existed between the verbal and nonverbal behaviors?

Answer the following questions about the interactions between the participants:
1. How did each person influence the other (i.e., as one became aggressive, did the other also become aggressive)?
2. How did you feel as you observed the interaction?
3. What were the most useful aspects of each person's behavior?
4. Which behaviors could be practiced?

Discuss your impressions with others who observed or engaged in the rehearsal. Answer the following questions:
1. What degree of consistency existed between the observer's rankings and those who rehearsed the scene?
2. Should the scene be rehearsed again?
3. How frequently might a situation like this occur during school conferences?
4. What questions or concerns have arisen?

A parent may have a specific verbal or nonverbal behavior(s) which is especially difficult to produce during interactions with school personnel. It can be helpful to identify such behaviors and practice them individually.

Check or write a behavior which you'd like to practice:

Verbal Behaviors

    _____ stating a fact
    _____ referring to a legislative regulation
    _____ asking a question
    _____ making a request
    _____ denying a request
    _____ making an empathetic remark
    _____ making a confronting statement
    _____ sharing a feeling
    _____ stating an opinion
    _____ other:

Nonverbal Behaviors

    _____ facing others
    _____ gazing directly at others
    _____ relaxing arms/hands
    _____ using appropriate gestures
    _____ maintaining appropriate facial expressions
    _____ showing consistency with verbal messages
    _____ other:

Use the worksheet on the next page to:

    _____ Engage in a behavioral rehearsal and practice at least one behavior.
    _____ Evaluate the behavioral rehearsal and discuss your performance with others.

WORKSHEET: BEHAVIORAL REHEARSAL

Describe the situation to be rehearsed.

Background or problem:

Participants: (I.e. teacher, psychologist, principal, others)

Engage in a behavioral rehearsal.

EVALUATE the behavioral rehearsal and discuss your behavior with others (Use the discussion guide on page 122.)

A process of self-evaluation, goal setting, and practice is necessary for continued growth and efficiency in parent behaviors. The following activities and related sets of questions may be used by the parent for such purposes:

Activity 1: Visualize yourself during a recent interaction involving school personnel.
- (a) What was your normal voice tone?
- (b) What kinds of messages did you present?
- (c) What types of body movements did you present?
- (d) How successful did you feel?
- (e) Should any of these be altered?

Activity 2: Visualize upcoming interactions with school personnel.
- (a) How would you like to look?
- (b) What would you like to say?
- (c) How would you like to feel?
- (d) What do you think will occur?
- (e) What would be the reaction of others?
- (f) What questions must be asked or answered?

Activity 3: Keep a journal or notes on your behavior during the next telephone or personnel interactions with school officials. Bring a recorder and tape the meeting.
- (a) What types of assertive statements did you make?
- (b) How frequently did you engage in such statements?
- (c) In what ways was your nonverbal and verbal behavior consistent or inconsistent?
- (d) How successful were the interactions?
- (e) What behaviors need to be practiced or improved?

Activity 4: Identify a future situation and plan methods of managing it.
- (a) What is a reasonable goal?
- (b) How will you cope with or manage tension or anxiety?
- (c) What behaviors need to be practiced?
- (d) What help is necessary?
- (e) How will you evaluate your own performance?

These activities are provided to help parents review and evaluate their previous behavior, envision and cope with possible problems, and begin systematically to prepare for a conference.

WORKSHEET

Use this page to record your answers to the questions posed for Activities 1-4 on page 125.

Conference Preparation

The parent's energy during a conference should focus on the program for the child. The more complete the planning prior to the conference, the more efficient the parent may be during the conference and the greater the energy he/she will have available for gaining or processing information and interacting with school personnel. The following checklist should be used as a guide prior to the conference:

Tasks begun	Tasks completed	
_____	_____	1. Review the child's current performance/behavior
_____	_____	look at the child's school work and social interactions
_____	_____	observe the child at home and at play
_____	_____	ask the child (if possible)
_____	_____	ask others (sibling, spouse, friends, teachers, physicians, psychologist)
_____	_____	ask yourself
_____	_____	collect necessary information (tests, work, etc.)
_____	_____	ask who is supposed to be monitoring and reporting on the child's progress.
_____	_____	(optional) ask to observe the child in class or in other school situations
_____	_____	2. Compare current performance to expectations and to past performance
_____	_____	review previous reports/records
_____	_____	identify positive or negative changes
_____	_____	look for patterns in specific areas
_____	_____	decide if your expectations have been realized
_____	_____	discuss reasons that expectations have or have not been realized
_____	_____	inquire about the meaning of test scores and reports
_____	_____	3. Identify questions or concerns

Tasks begun	Tasks completed	
_____	_____	4. Optional: Review legal rights
_____	_____	read state and federal rules and regulations
_____	_____	(optional) refer to the state plan and school district plan
_____	_____	(required) discuss questions about legal rights with other parents, advocates, or professionals
_____	_____	5. Review possible programs for your child that are currently available within your school district
_____	_____	ask to visit or observe program options being considered for your child
_____	_____	call parent organizations, refer to school district consultants
_____	_____	6. Ask other parents about their feelings regarding the effectiveness of teachers and support personnel who will be providing services to your child (re: special education teacher, speech therapist, reading consultant)
_____	_____	7. Generate suggestions and additional problems, questions, or concerns. (optional) Bring a tape recorder.
_____	_____	8. Seek, aid, or gain additional information or request an individual to accompany you to a conference
_____	_____	advocate
_____	_____	legal counsel
_____	_____	independent psychological evaluators
_____	_____	medical personnel
_____	_____	babysitters
_____	_____	parent groups
_____	_____	friends
_____	_____	clergymen

Tasks begun	Tasks completed	
_____	_____	9. Request or confirm conference arrangement with school personnel
_____	_____	return or initiate telephone calls
_____	_____	speak to the appropriate personnel
_____	_____	select and note date, time, and location
_____	_____	request written notice
_____	_____	discuss purpose and length of conference
_____	_____	share questions and concerns
_____	_____	notify school personnel about persons who will accompany you
_____	_____	inquire about materials or reports which you should bring
_____	_____	arrange, if necessary, to review your child's folder or reports
_____	_____	10. Collect and arrange materials and prepare yourself psychologically
_____	_____	collect materials such as reports, letters, old tests, paper, and pencils
_____	_____	include items such as cigarettes, gum or candy to use during breaks
_____	_____	put records and notes into labeled folders or notebooks
_____	_____	outline possible strategies to cope with problems
_____	_____	set up an agenda of items and a possible time schedule
_____	_____	identify the person(s) next to whom you'd like to sit
_____	_____	identify behaviors or situations to practice
_____	_____	schedule a time to practice and an individual with whom to practice and join feedback
_____	_____	buy new batteries and tapes if the conference is to be recorded.

A parent who has completed all these tasks prior to the conference, and who has some experience with the other persons attending the conference will face no surprises during the conference itself. Indeed, the highly skilled parent will be able to predict in advance exactly what will take place during the conference and plan his/her responses accordingly.

WORKSHEET: CONFERENCE PREPARATION

What are your major questions or goals?

In what ways to you want to act assertively?

How do you want others to act towards you?

What compromises might you accept?

What were the results?

Conference Review

Following a conference, the parent should file notes, review events, and evaluate the general success of meetings. The more efficient the post conference evaluation and summary, the greater the likelihood that the parent/child can benefit from the outcomes of the conference.

Some conferences will be disasterous. The parent's responsibility in such cases is to identify conditions and behaviors which precipitated or aggravated negative behaviors. The task is to avoid such conditions during the next conference and to influence future conferences towards more productive interactions. The following checklist should be used as a guide after the conference:

___ 1. Required: Reread notes, fill in missing information, edit.
___ 2. Required: File notes in a notebook or in a dated, labeled folder.
___ 3. Write follow-up letters.
___ 4. Arrange for additional meetings.
___ 5. Discuss outcomes with another person.
___ 6. Plan new goals.

Summary

A great deal of determination and work is required to become more assertive during interactions with school personnel. However, such commitment is often necessary for parents of handicapped children since the education and welfare of their children is at stake. Parents must be firm in affirming the rights afforded to themselves and to their children as human beings and as established by legal and legislative procedures.

Assertiveness alone is not the answer. Knoweldge, research, homework, and judgment go hand in hand with assertiveness. The more parents know and the more skills they develop, the more they can persuasively discuss the issues.

Practicing assertive verbal and nonverbal behaviors alone, with a partner, or with a group can enhance the parent's assertive skills and insure that such skills are employed, when and if necessary, with school personnel.

Systematic conference preparation will help insure that important information and materials are collected and available. Hopefully, such preparation will assist that parent to be organized and ready to interact with school personnel and to cope with problems that inevitably arise.

CONCLUSION

Assertive skills are but one part of a total set of skills required by parents to participate effectively in the educational planning for their handicapped child.

For some people, assertiveness comes quite easily, but for most it does not. Our society tends to value non-assertion, and since most of us care very much what others think of us we are likely to act in ways that bring their approval. We have seen assertiveness in others interpreted as rudeness and selfishness. We do not want our own behavior to be interpreted this way. We do not want to be viewed negatively.

In a large, complex society like ours, however, assertiveness is often a necessary element of survival and for parents of handicapped children, assertiveness is absolutely necessary in order to serve as an effective advocate for the child.

It is difficult for people to change familiar ways of acting and responding. Both discomfort and anxiety can arise in changing old ways to new. Parents might make the transition from non-assertion to assertion more easily if they seriously considered and enumerated the negative and positive consequences of each. What are the possible consequences of acting assertively in the future? What are the consequences of past, non-assertive behavior?

Possible negative consequences of non-assertion and assertion:

Non-Assertion	Assertion
child gets poor program and/or no program at all	teacher takes anger out on your child
you get angry and/or eventually lose your temper	people at school talk about you negatively
you feel depressed and/or anxious	teacher or principal gets angry with you

Affirming one's right frequently involves taking risks, but these risks may be no greater than the risk of outbursts of anger created by the frustration of non-assertion. The parent may think that by remaining silent and by not taking action, he or she is assuming no risk: by not disturbing the teacher, the parent insures that nothing bad will happen to the child. If as a result, however, an inappropriate plan is implemented or no plan is designed or presented at all, then the child will not receive adequate services. These are negative and long-term consequences, although they may not be immediately apparent.

In thinking about changing behavior and being more assertive, parents might find it helpful to view the situation in terms of a balance of consequences. All behaviors have consequences. It is important to look at the positive and negative consequences of each type of behavior for particular situations. This type of pre-planning and systematic thinking may make parents more aware of the problem and the possible alternatives. As a result, the situation becomes more controllable.

Case Study

I wish I could say to you that everything is great, Susie is great, her teacher is great, her program is great. But you know that isn't really so. Maybe nothing will ever be good enough for me. However, I do feel that at this point Susie is progressing very well and that her teacher really cares about her. The teacher and I have had several good conferences about Susie's program, and I am constantly pleased at how much Susie's teacher values my suggestions. Sometimes, of course, I do get negative reports from school. I suppose I always will. They don't upset me as much as they did, although I must admit that those guilty feelings still tend to come back. And I do hesitate to question or criticize something that concerns me – especially now when things are going so well in general. However, after weighing the consequences I feel more able to judge whether I should say something or not. And the teacher, bless her, has been very accepting of my questioning. She has often had the same concerns.

I really think we are all doing as much for Susie as is humanly possible.

It is important to note that I feel most successful as an advocate for other parents and children. I have been able to help parents become more open and direct in their interactions with school personnel. In advance, after agreeing on our goals, we discuss and plan the conference, decide on our strategy, and try to predict the school's responses. After the conference we feel that we have contributed to the plan, even if many of our suggestions were not incorporated. We feel more controlled and productive. Even when we lose on an issue, if we have predicted the possible losses and have managed our tensions, we feel we've gained. We can say, "win some, lose some," and look toward the future with optimism. At least we're in there as participants.

We're parents who are seen and heard!

APPENDIX A

Answer Key

Part I. ASSERTIVE BEHAVIOR

Exercise
1. b
2. a
3. b
4. b
5. b
6. a
7. a
8. a
9. a
10. b
11. a
12. c

Part II. VERBAL BEHAVIORS

Verbal Behavior – Scripts A-L

Exercise 13, Script A

1. c. aggressive
2. a. anger
3. a. insulting
4. b. discontinue

Exercise 14, Script B

1. c. assertive
2. b. challenge
3. a. sharing feelings
4. a. continue discussion

Exercise 15, Script C

1. a. aggressive
2. a. anger and blame
3. b. discontinue

Part II. VERBAL BEHAVIORS (Continued)

Exercise 16, Script D

    1. c. assertive

    2. a. empathic, requesting

    3. a. increase

Exercise 17, Script E

    1. a. nonassertive

    2. b. intimidation

    3. b. decrease

Exercise 18, Script F

    1. a. assertive

    2. b. empathic, positive

    3. b. increase

Exercise 19, Script G

    1. a. too soft

    2. b. too slow

    3. b. nonassertive

Exercise 20, Script H

    1. a. too high

    2. a. too loud

    3. c. aggressive

Exercise 21, Script I

    1. b. noncredible

    2. I do not wish to consider that alternative.

Exercise 22, Script J

    1. a. assertive

    2. a. assertive

Exercise 23, Script K

    1. a. assertive

    2. b. aggressive

    3. b. inconsistent

    4. a. too fast

       c. too much stress on some words (e.g., my, your)

Part II. VERBAL BEHAVIORS (Continued)

Exercise 24, Script L

- 1. a. assertive
- 2. c. nonassertive
- 3. a. inconsistent
- 4. a. uneven stress
  - b. stammering
  - c. tone of voice (whining)

Exercise 25, Script M

- 1. a. positive
- 2. b. negative
- 3. b. inconsistency

Exercise 26: Possible responses--

Although you always speak to me in a polite and concerned manner, my son is not receiving educational services.

Part III. NONVERBAL BEHAVIORS

Exercise
- 28. b
- 29. b
- 30. b
- 31. b
- 32. a
- 33. a
- 34. b
- 35. b
- 36. a
- 37. a
- 38. b
- 39. a
- 40. a
- 41. b
- 42. b
- 43. b
- 44. a

45. a

> Possible Parent Response: It would make me feel more comfortable if you would look at me when I am discussing my ideas.

46. b

> Possible Parent Response: I understand that you are trying to emphasize a point, but I feel angry when you point your finger at me.

Part IV. LISTENING BEHAVIORS

Exercise 47. b

48. Possible questions to be asked by parent:
    - Can you explain this program?
    - Have you heard of this technique?
    - Will you give some additional information about this approach?
    - In what ways could we use this technique?

49. a

50. What do the scores mean?

    What progress has been made?

51. Some questions a parent might ask:
    - What are Peter's needs? How are they similar to the needs of autistic children?
    - Will you place Peter in a program designed for autistic children?
    - What does the statement "Peter's miserable life" mean?
    - What does the term "differential diagnosis" mean?
    - What alternatives does the school suggest?
    - What alternatives does the psychologist suggest?

52. b

53. b

54. b (speaker's name)

55. b (program options)

56. What program options are available?

57.

| What are the results of testing? | Psychologist- | educable, reading 2.5, math 4.0 |
| | Needs skills- | money, math, handwriting |

58.

| What are the options for Kelly? | Psychologist- | further testing for learning full time school program: typing, English, swimming, math, part time job/part time work (He doen't think she's ready for this.) |

59.

	principal	psychologist	teacher	parent
What's the most important problem?	Schedule conflict	Testing for learning disabilities	Lack of motivation	Handling money
What has been done this year?		Counseling	Unit on	Not much

60. any answer
61. a
62. b
63. b
64. a
65. b
66. a
67. a
68. a

Part V.   LEGISLATION

Exercise
69. b
70. a
71. b   is not
72. b   is not
73. The school is responsible for transportation to and from school. What do you suggest?
74. a   shows awareness
75. b   is not
76. a 3,   b 1,   c 2
77. b, c, e
78. I will be bringing a friend. I am allowed to bring an individual at my discretion.
79. It was my impression that parents were to be involved in the design of the I.E.P. I want to be present at discussions involving Jim's plan. Let's meet next week.
80. a, c
81. a, b, c, d
82. b
83. c, d
84. When will Seth be having speech therapy and music?
85. d, b, c
86. The law indicates that the school must be accessible to a child if that is the best placement. Or: We think something temporary can be set up until you get the permanent structures built, you have three years.
87. You must give me the opportunity to benefit from your class as others do.

   I understand that it's difficult but teachers are now expected to make such arrangements.
88. b, c
89. a
90. a
91. b
92. a

140

Part VI. PROBLEMS & STRATEGIES

Exercise
93. a, b
94. a, c
95. b, c, d
96. b
97. a
98. b, a, c
99. a, b, a, c
100. c, b, a
101. b
102. a
103. b
104. a, d, e, f
105. a, b, d
106. a
107. I feel a bit anxious.
108. 1. b, 2. b, 3. a, 4. b, 5. a
109. This is a problem which I planned for. I know it will be difficult, but I will handle it.
110. a. Probably not happiness

   b. State feelings; state plans

   c. Look at an advocate or friend for support. Take several deep breathes.

   d. I feel concerned at this point. I don't think everything is all right.

   I'd like to review the last few suggestions that were made.

111. a. Probably not relief

   b. Continue or set up another conference

   c. Suggest a one minute break. Stretch and flex your muscles.

   d. At this point I am feeling very frustrated.

   e. I understand your concern but the final decision about whether he lives at home, is ours. Billy is entitled to an education and an education in the least restrictive environment. A state facility does not seem to be a good choice.

112. b

113. I will be taking Johnny to Children's Hospital for an evaluation next month.

Part VI.   PROBLEMS & STRATEGIES (Continued)

Exercise   114. a

115. a

116. b

117. a. is not
     b. sign

118. a

119. a. was being protected
     b. should be silent at this time

120. a. are
     b. needs not

121. b

122. c, a, b

123. b, c, a

124. b, a, c

125. - I would like to know what skills he needs help with and what you would suggest I can do at home. (Direct request)

   - I understand that you feel he will grow out of this but I am concerned. What reading services are available? (Shared feelings, direct request)

126. - Is it something bad? I'm really not up to handling that sort of thing today. (Direct, honest statement of feeling)

127. - I feel angry with that statement. My son is entitled to a full morning of school. (Statement of feeling, statement of right)

   - I understand that you want George in class for one hour, but I want him to remain the entire time like the rest of the class. (Empathic, request)

128. b

129. b, d, a

130. I would like to discuss Susie's program. I have some questions about reading. She doesn't seem to be progressing.

131. I am entitled to make suggestions.

132. What are some of the good things that my child can do?

REFERENCES

LEGISLATION, RULES AND REGULATIONS

P.L. 94-142 The Education for all Handicapped Children Act of 1975. Federal Register, August 23, 1977.

Section 504 of the Rehabilitation Act of 1973. Federal Register, May 4, 1977.

The Family Educational Rights and Privacy Act of 1974. Federal Register, February 27, 1976.

Martin, R., Educating Handicapped Children: The Legal Mandate, Champaign, Ill., Research Press, 1979.

ASSERTIVENESS

Alberti, R. E. and Emmons, M. L., Stand Up, Speak Out, Talk Back. New York: Pocket Books, 1975.

Alberti, R. E. and Emmons, M. L., Your Perfect Right: A Guide to Assertive Behavior. San Luis Obispo: Impact Publishers, Third Revised Edition, 1978.

Ascaer, L. M., Phillips, D., "Guided Behavior Rehearsal" Behavior Therapy and Experimental Psychiatry. Pergamon Press, Vol. 6, pp. 215-218, 1975.

Bloom, L. Z., Coburn, K., and Pearlman, J., The New Assertive Woman. New York: Dell Books, 1975.

Cotler, S. B. and Guerra, J. J., Assertion Training. Research Press, 1976.

Ellis, A. and Harper, R., A New Guide to Rational Living. No. Hollywood, California: Wilshire Book Company, 1975.

Eisler, R. M., Miller, P. M. and Hersen, M., Components of Assertive Behavior, Journal of Clinical Psychology, 1973, 29, 3, 295-299.

Eisler, R. M., Hersen, M. and Miller, P.M., Effects of Modeling on Components of Assertive Behavior. Journal of Behavior Therapy and Experimental Psychiatry, 1973, 4, 1-6.

Fielder, D., Beach, L. R., On the Decision to Be Assertive. Journal of Consulting and Clinical Psychology.

Fensterheim, H. and Baer, J. Don't Say Yes When You Want to Say No. New York: Dell Publishing Company, 1975.

Freidman, P. H., The Effects of Modeling and Role-playing on Assertive Behavior. In R. Rubin, H. Fensterheim, H. Lazarus, and C. Franks (Eds.), Advances in Behavior Therapy, New York: Academic Press, 1971, 149-169.

Goldstein, A. P., Martens, Jr., Hubben, J., Van Belle, H. A., Schaff, W., Wiersma, H. and Goldhart, A., The Use of Modeling to Increase Independent Behavior. Behavior Research and Therapy, 1973, 11, 31-42.

Hersen, M., Eisler, R. M. and Miller, P. M., Development of Assertive Responses, Behavior Research and Therapy, 1973, 11, 505-521.

Jakubowski-Spector, P., Facilitating the Growth of Women Through Assertive Training, The Counseling Psychologist, 1973, 4, 1, 75-86.

Jakubowski-Spector, P., An Introduction to Assertive Training Procedures for Women. Washington, D.C.: American Personnel and Guidance Association, 1973.

Kazdin, A. Effects of Covert Modeling and Model Reinforcement on Assertive Behavior. Journal of Abnormal Psychology, 1974, Vol. 83, No. 3, 240-252.

Lange, A. J. and Jakubowski, T., Responsible Assertive Behavior. Champaign, Illinois: Research Press, 1976.

Lazarus, A. A., Behavior Therapy and Beyond. New York: McGraw-Hill, 1971.

Liberman, R. P., King, L. W., DeRisi, W. J., McCann, M., Personal Effectiveness. Champaign, Illinois: Research Press, 1975.

McFall, R. M. and Lillesand, D. B., Behavior Rehearsal with Modeling and Coaching in Assertion Training. Journal of Abnormal Psychology, 1971, 77, 313-323.

McFall, R. M. and Marston, A. R., An Experimental Investigation of Behavior Research in Assertive Training. Journal of Abnormal Psychology, 1970, 76, 295-303.

McFall, R. M. and Twentyman, C. T., Four Experiments on the Relative Contributions of Rehearsal, Modeling, and Coaching to Assertive Training. Journal of Abnormal Psychology, 1973, 81, 199-218.

Melnick, J., and Stocker, R. B., An Experimental Analysis of the Behavioral Rehearsal with Feedback Technique in Assertiveness Training. Behavior Therapy, 8, 222-228, 1977.

Newman, D. R., Using Assertive Training. In J. C. Krumboltz and C. E. Thoresen (Eds.), Behavioral Counseling. New York: Holtz, Reinhart and Winston, 1969, 433-441.

Rathus, S. A., An Experimental Investigation of Assertive Training in a Group Setting. Journal of Behavior Therapy and Experimental Psychiatry, 1972, 3, 179-183.

Rathus, S. A., Instigation of Assertive Behavior Through Video Tape--Mediated Assertive Models and Directed Practice. Behavioral Research and Therapy, 1973, 11, 57-65.

Salter, A., Conditioned Reflex Therapy. New York: Farrar Straus, 1949.

Serber, M. Teaching the Nonverbal Components of Assertive Training. Journal of Behavior Therapy and Experimental Psychiatry, 1972, 3, 179-183.

Wolfe, J. L., Fodor, I. G., Modifying Assertive Behavior in Women: A Comparison of Three Approaches. Behavior Therapy, 8, 567-574, 1977.

Wolpe, Joseph, Psychotherapy by Reciprocal Inhibition. Stanford, California: Stanford University Press, 1958.

Wolpe, J. and Lazarus, A. A., Behavior Therapy Techniques: A Guide to the Treatment of Neuroses. Oxford: Pergamon, 1966.

Wolpe, Joseph, The Practice of Behavior Therapy. New York: Pergamon Press, 1969.

PARENTS

Blatt, B., Biklen, D., Bogdan, R., An Alternative Textbook in Special Education. Denver, Colorado, Love Publishing Company, 1977.

Brown, S. L., Moersch, M. S., Eds., Parents on the Team. Ann Arbor, Michigan, the University of Michigan Press, P,O. Box 1104.

Buscaglia, Leo, The Disabled and Their Parents: A Counseling Challenge. New Jersey: Charles B. Slack, Inc., 1975.

Cain, L. F., "Parent Groups: Their Role in a Better Life for the Handicapped." Exceptional Child, May, 1976.

Chin, P. C., Winn, J., Waltees, R. H., Two-Way Talking with Parents of Special Children. St. Louis, The C. V. Mosby Company, 1978.

Clements, J. E., Alexander, R. N., Parent Learning: Bringing It All Back Home, Focus on Exceptional Children. Line Publishing Company, Vol. 7, #5, October, 1975.

Closer Look, Fall, 1977, National Information Center for the Handicapped, P.O. Box 1492, Washington, D.C.

Cooper, J. O., Edge, D., *Parenting: Strategies and Educational Methods*. Columbus, Ohio, Charles E. Merrill Publishing Company, 1978.

Dempsey, John, Ed., *Community Services for Retarded Children, the Consumer-Provided Relationship*. The University Press, 1975.

Farber, B., Lewis, M., "The Symbolic Use of Parents, A Sociological Critique of Educational Practice." *Journal of Research and Development in Education*, 1975, 8, 34-42.

Gordon, I. J., Breivogel, W. F., *Building Effective Home-School Relationships*. Boston, MA, Allyn and Bacon, 1976.

Gordon, S., *Living Fully: A Guide for Young People with A Handicap, their Parents, their Teachers, and Professionals*. New York, The John Day Company, 1975.

Gordon, T., *Parent Effectiveness Training*. New York: Peter H. Wyden, Publisher, 1970.

Gorham, Kathryn A., "A Lost Generation of Parents." *Exceptional Children*, May, 1975.

Greenbaum, J., Parents' Attitudes Towards Mainstreaming Their Own Handicapped Child. Ann Arbor, Michigan, Unpublished Doctoral Dissertation, University of Michigan, (in press).

Keniston, K. and the Carnegie Council on Children, *All Our Children, the American Family Under Pressure*. Harcourt, Brace, Jovanovich, 1977.

Kroth, R., Scholl, G., *Getting Schools Involved with Parents*. Reston, Virginia, Council for Exceptional Children, 1978.

Kroth, R., "Parents--Powerful and Necessary Allies." *Teaching Exceptional Children*, Spring, 1978.

Kroth, R. L., *Communicating with Parents of Exceptional Children: Improving Parent-Teacher Relationships*. Denver, Colorado, Love Publishing Company, 1975.

Kroth, R. L., Simpson, R. L., *Parent Conferences as a Teaching Strategy*. Denver, Colorado, Love Publishing Co., 1975.

Losen, R., *Parent Conferences in Schools*. Rockleigh, New Jersey, Allyn and Bacon, Inc., 1977.

Markel, G., Ed. *The Impact and Implications of State and Federal Legislation Effecting the Handicapped*. Ann Arbor, Michigan, Institute Proceedings, University of Michigan, 1977.

Stewart, J., *Counseling Parents of Exceptional Children*. Columbus, Ohio, Charles E. Merrill Publishing Co., 1978.

Turnbull, H. R., Turnbull, A., *Free Appropriate Public Education, Law and Implementation*. Denver, Colorado, Love Publishing Co., 1978.

Turnbull, A. P., Turnbull, H., *Parents Speak Out*. Columbus, Ohio, Charles E. Merrill Publishing Company, 1978

Wolfensberger, W., and K. Richard, Ed., *Management of the Family of the Mentally Retarded*. Chicago, Illinois, Follett Educational Corporation, 1969.

Yoshida, R., Fenton, K., Kaufman, M., Maxwell, J., "Parent Involvement in the Special Education Pupil Planning Process: The School's Perspective." *Exceptional Children*, April, 1978.

ABOUT THE AUTHORS

Geraldine Markel Ph.D. is on the faculty of the Special Education Program at the University of Michigan School of Education. Previously, she has worked with emotionally disturbed and learning disabled children and youth. She has functioned as a teacher, high school reading consultant, Director of the Children's Division of the U of M Reading and Learning Skills Center, as an evaluation consultant for the Ann Arbor Public Schools and as an editor at the U of M Division of Management Education's programmed learning workshop. She is the parent of three children.

Dr. Markel has presented numerous workshops at state and local conferences and has developed interests in behavior modification, competency based instruction and programmed learning.

Judith Greenbaum is the parent of four children, the youngest of whom is retarded. She is a member of the board of several parent-professional organizations for handicapped children. In addition, she is a community leader and advocate for the rights of handicapped children and their families. Mrs. Greenbaum is also a doctoral candidate and instructor in the Special Education Program of the University of Michigan School of Education.

Her current area of research is on attitudes, expectations and preferences of parents of handicapped children regarding school placement of their children; in particular, the mainstreaming placement. As an educator she has often lectured on this topic.

With Dr. Markel, she has presented workshops and developed materials on assertiveness skills and self management for parents and school personnel.